Dynamic Principles of Professional Development

Dynamic Principles of Professional Development

Essential Elements of Effective Teacher Preparation

Edited by Caroline M. Crawford
and Sandra L. Hardy

ROWMAN & LITTLEFIELD
Lanham • Boulder • New York • London

Published by Rowman & Littlefield
A wholly owned subsidiary of The Rowman & Littlefield Publishing Group, Inc.
4501 Forbes Boulevard, Suite 200, Lanham, Maryland 20706
www.rowman.com

Unit A, Whitacre Mews, 26–34 Stannary Street, London SE11 4AB

Copyright © 2017 by Caroline M. Crawford and Sandra L. Hardy

All rights reserved. No part of this book may be reproduced in any form or by any electronic or mechanical means, including information storage and retrieval systems, without written permission from the publisher, except by a reviewer who may quote passages in a review.

British Library Cataloguing in Publication Information Available

Library of Congress Cataloging-in-Publication Data Is Available

ISBN 978-1-4758-3920-3 (cloth: alk. paper)
ISBN 978-1-4758-3921-0 (pbk: alk. paper)
ISBN 978-1-4758-3922-7 (electronic)

Printed in the United States of America

Contents

Foreword — vii
Nancy P. Gallavan

Preface — xi

Acknowledgments — xiii

Editors' Note — xvii
Caroline M. Crawford and Sandra L. Hardy

Introduction — xix
Caroline M. Crawford and Sandra L. Hardy

Overview and Framework — xxv
Caroline M. Crawford and Sandra L. Hardy

1 Mentors as Associated Teacher Educators: Inquiry as Professional Development — 1
   Stacey Pylman, Randi Stanulis, and Lindsay Joseph Wexler

2 Transforming Induction: Contexts and Practice — 17
   Sandra L. Hardy

3 Teachers Learning Together at Auburn Elementary: Supporting Classroom Teachers as Associated Teacher Educators — 37
   Cynthia Carver, Marcia Hudson, Molly Abbott, Sarah Bruha, Colleen Bugaj, Jennifer Johnson, and Serena Stock

4 Promoting ATE Standards for Professional Development in
Pre-K Settings   59
Noran L. Moffett, Melanie M. Frizzell, Yolanda Brownlee-Williams, Stacye A. Blount, and Nurah-Talibah N. Moffett

5 Teacher Educators as Collegial Mentors: Integrating Instructional Technologies through an Extended Community of Practice Professional Development Approach   77
Caroline M. Crawford

Afterword   99
Caroline M. Crawford and Sandra L. Hardy

About the Editors   103

About the Contributors   105

Foreword

Serving as the president of the Association of Teacher Educators (ATE) includes the privilege of appointing one or two Commissions to guide the association with topics and issues in education. This privilege is accompanied with the responsibility of identifying particular areas of importance and/or concern as well as inviting interested members to participate on the Commissions.

Commissions allow ATE members to meet regularly to discuss research and practices followed by opportunities to disseminate presentations and publications. By delving into multiple perspectives associated with a particular area and deliberating the impact on teacher education, Commission members help inform and support both the actions of ATE and contribute to the research literature grounding teacher education.

The ATE Commission on Classroom Teachers as Associated Teacher Educators is one Commission that I joyously appointed in 2013 as I began my ATE presidency. My vision for this Commission was to consider the research and resources available to classroom teachers and that ATE can promote combined with the technological avenues that ATE can establish to strengthen the educational preparation of our vital partners in teacher education found in the field.

I greatly value the expertise of classroom teachers, the energies they dedicate to their learners, and the experiences they provide in the preparation of classroom teachers; appointing this Commission allowed me to empower and equip teacher educators both at universities and in classrooms. Establishing this Commission sparked the conversations to revisit the origin of ATE and the contributions to education given that ATE began in 1920 as the National Association of Directors of Supervised Student Teaching.

I believe that teacher education involves the aligned messages, modeling, methods, and mentoring from two significant sources: (a) expert university instructors and well-developed courses in teacher education and (b) experienced P-12 teachers and classrooms in a variety of content subject areas, educational settings, and diverse communities. Sound research and accrediting agencies have long rationalized that teacher preparation requires strong partnerships between university instructors and classroom teachers.

My aim was to select a group of ATE members ascribing to this belief. Plus, my own career resonates the reciprocity shared between the university and the classroom; I have evolved from an undergraduate education candidate who prepared to be a classroom teacher, an intern in the classroom, a novice teacher, a graduate student teacher leader, a classroom intern mentor, and a doctoral candidate to a teacher educator, an intern supervisor, and a teacher educator preparing future doctoral teacher educators. Therefore, appointing this ATE Commission was a natural reflection of my life's work and meaningful decision for the ATE.

For many years, educators have faced an unresolved dilemma in teacher preparation. Many teacher preparation personnel and programs grapple with the dynamics involved in their partnerships with school administrators and classroom teachers. Likewise, many school administrators and classroom teachers wrestle with the expectations in their partnerships with universities and interns. Everyone agrees that new classroom teachers must be prepared by qualified teacher educators for ever-changing educational contexts. However, only through a seamless partnership specifying the purposes of each participant in the preparation of teachers will the intern, P-12 learners, classroom teachers, educational systems, and teacher preparation benefit.

As an educator who has evolved from a classroom teacher to a university instructor, I am fully aware of one overarching concern. Frequently, when classroom teachers are asked to mentor a university teacher preparation intern, the classroom teachers do not view themselves as teacher educators nor do they approach mentoring as an opportunity contributing to their personal growth, professional development, and pedagogical expertise.

Too often, classroom teachers respond to the request to mentor interns as another task consuming their time, energy, and sometimes, their money. Revisiting the purposes and practices of a seamless partnership between the teacher preparation program and the P-12 school poses five specific benefits for the classroom teacher that may influence teacher preparation processes and outcomes.

BENEFIT ONE

While mentoring a university teacher preparation intern, the classroom teacher has the rare opportunity to view individual practices through the eyes of another professional in a nonthreatening environment. Few professions offer this type of chance to reflect critically on one's own practices then to modify and advance practices appropriately. Most teachers think about improving their practices as if someone were watching; mentoring an intern transforms thoughts into authentic outcomes.

BENEFIT TWO

While transforming thoughts into authentic actions, the classroom teacher can develop mechanisms to enhance teacher self-efficacy. Most classroom teachers who are asked to mentor an intern demonstrate proficiencies to guide and support an apprentice. These proficiencies indicate that the classroom teacher has developed the confidence and competence to affect and promote student learning with comfort and care for the learner and the teacher. The opportunity to mentor an intern encompasses the optimal professional development.

BENEFIT THREE

While optimizing professional development, the classroom teacher also has the opportunity to transform personal growth and pedagogical expertise. As a mentor, the classroom teacher may realize the individual benefits from the passage of time and the discoveries from experience. These insights provide the intern with the most valuable perceptions that the intern will glean and take into her or his own career. The keen classroom teacher recognizes these unique and astute moments for one generation to shape future generations.

BENEFIT FOUR

While shaping future generations, the classroom teacher not only gains in pedagogical expertise, but the classroom teacher also increases acumen into andragogical practices. University interns are adults aspiring to become classroom teachers. Although the classroom teacher mentor and the university intern are focused on advancing their pedagogical expertise to increase the engagement and achievement of their students, the relationship between the mentor and the intern centers on andragogical practices related to the teaching, learning, and schooling of adults.

Knowles (1980, 1984) identified five characteristics of andragogy essential for the education of adults: (a) adults are moving from dependency to self-directedness; (b) experiences accumulate into resourcefulness; (c) readiness to learn is oriented as developmental tasks of social roles; (d) perspectives change from postponed or future use to immediate application accompanied with a shift from subject centeredness to problem centeredness; and (e) motivation becomes internal rather external.

BENEFIT FIVE

Consequently, while experiencing the transformation of the intern, the classroom teacher is also experiencing transformation in ways that benefit the teacher, the students, the school, and the community. Many classroom teachers who mentor interns discover new horizons in education prompting them to pursue additional endorsements, advanced degrees, and new career choices such as university teacher educators. Unlike the teaching, learning, and schooling associated with P-12 students, mentoring interns offers classroom teachers with new, perhaps endless, possibilities. I certainly can attest that this series of transformations influenced my career.

CONCLUDING THOUGHTS

I am excited that the members of the ATE Commission on Classroom Teachers as Associated Teacher Educators have authored these texts. Shepherded by the Commission co-chairs, Caroline M. Crawford and Sandra L. Hardy have assembled a fascinating collection of outstanding research and principles in these texts applicable to teacher preparation, professional development, and learning communities.

These insightful chapters provide well-developed purposes and practices contributing to the roles, responsibilities, and rigor of classroom teachers who mentor interns in their transformation as teacher educators and partners in the preparation of teachers. I greatly appreciate the dedication of this text's coeditors and all of the authors who have contributed to its success.

—**Nancy P. Gallavan**,
Association of Teacher Educators President 2013–2014

REFERENCES

Knowles, M. (1980). *The modern practice of adult education: From pedagogy to andragogy*. Wilton, CN: Association Press.
Knowles, M. (1984). *Andragogy in action*. San Francisco, CA: Jossey-Bass.

Preface

The Association of Teacher Educators (ATE) Commission on Classroom Teachers as Associated Teacher Educators brings forth three distinct yet related texts:

> The first text, *Redefining Teacher Preparation: Learning from Experience in Educator Development,* highlights applications and reflections of Associated Teacher Educator (ATE) Standards and offers conceptual frameworks and contextual realities in connections to classroom educators at all stages of their career.
>
> The second text, *Dynamic Principles of Professional Development: Essential Elements of Effective Teacher Preparation* focuses upon differentiated elements toward inquiry and the reflectivity of practitioners as dynamic components of professional development.
>
> The third text, *Teacher to Teacher Mentality: Purposeful Practice in Teacher Education,* focuses upon professional discourse that revolves around induction efforts resulting from educators working together to inform one another's practice.

ASSOCIATION OF TEACHER EDUCATORS

Association of Teacher Educators (ATE) promotes advocacy, equity, leadership, and professionalism for classroom teachers as associated teacher educators in all settings and supports quality education and collegial support for all learners at all levels. An understanding of the ATE Commission on Classroom Teachers as Associated Teacher Educators may be framed through the innovative efforts of Dr. Nancy Gallavan, ATE past president, as her insightful vast understandings of teacher education transformations led to the realization of this Commission.

The ATE Commission on Classroom Teachers as Associated Teacher Educators (active from 2013 through 2016) has been productively engaged in enriching discussions and cutting-edge efforts, not only through a theoretical and research focus but also through the attainment of classroom teacher input. As such, this text reflects the Commission's efforts guided by the Commission's vision and mission concerning the current state of classroom teachers as associated teacher educators and future developments in that regard.

COMMISSION VISION

The ATE Commission on Classroom Teachers as Associated Teacher Educators promotes advocacy, equity, leadership, and professionalism for classroom teachers as associated teacher educators in all settings and supports quality education and collegial support for all learners at all levels and contexts.

COMMISSION MISSION

The ATE Commission on Classroom Teachers as Associated Teacher Educators advocates quality teacher education through exemplary collaborative efforts and collegial understandings that reflect the inherent importance of classroom teachers as associated teacher educators.

ATE past president Nancy Gallavan (2013–2014) has described the charge of the ATE Commission on Classroom Teachers as Associated Teacher Educators to include the consideration of the research and resources available to classroom teachers. Further the Commission's mission recognizes that ATE promotes, combined with the technological avenues, the ATE establishment of informative and supportive vital educational preparation of partners in the field.

With the esteemed group of Commission colleagues that Dr. Gallavan coalesced, the Commission brings forward meaningful ideas for projects, research endeavors, publication efforts, as well as considerations toward enhancing grant funded areas of focus. The Commission further recognizes ATE as a primary resource through which to obtain high-quality professional development opportunities, with special emphasis upon classroom teachers as associated teacher educators to mentor and guide candidates, novice classroom teachers, and colleagues.

Acknowledgments

CAROLINE M. CRAWFORD

There are so many colleagues who have been involved in the success of this text. I would like to first acknowledge the Association of Teacher Educators (ATE) as a truly extraordinary professional organization. The professionals within this organization live, breathe, and forever journey through strengthening the profession of teacher education. Through the ATE, I have been honored to meet, work with, and forever have been impacted by truly extraordinary teacher educators, who have supported my understanding within the field as well as developed a sense of a welcoming family among our ATE membership.

I would like to begin this discussion through an acknowledgment of my deep respect and collegial admiration for Dr. Nancy P. Gallavan. Her trust and belief in my abilities led toward this opportunity to chair the Association of Teacher Educators (ATE) Commission on Classroom Teachers as Associated Teacher Educators that occurred from 2013 through 2016. These 3 years were an amazing experience and quite a learning journey, for which I will always be grateful.

I would also like to bring forward my appreciation for our many colleagues who engaged in our Commission on Classroom Teachers as Associated Teacher Educators as committee members who engaged in our mission quite selflessly. Each committee member brought forward their own professional strengths, qualities, and pleasant creativity as we progressed forward toward realizing our Commission's successes. The strength of understanding and depth of respect for professional classroom teacher colleagues was inherent in each undertaking and realized within each of the Commission's successes.

I would like to state my respect for the amazing talents that each of our Committee Member colleagues brought forward toward supporting our mission, as well as the thoughtful efforts recognized within each demanding undertaking. The Commission membership has every reason to reflect a level of accomplishment throughout our Commission experience, as our years together have not only strengthened our professional understandings but also added fundamental and essential work to the professional knowledge base.

I would also like to acknowledge and deeply thank Dr. Sandra L. Hardy for being such an integral part of our text as an integral coeditor, as well as fundamentally important in our Commission's success. Thank you for always being professional, amazingly supportive, always going so far above and beyond all of my hopes for support, and for reflecting your true self as a proficient, skilled, knowledgeable, generous, kind, and caring professional. This text would not have been realized without your depth of engagement throughout our journey.

A truly amazing faculty advisor, mentor, and ultimate teacher educator is a rare gem of a professional. This describes Dr. Allen R. Warner, professor emeritus, from the University of Houston in Houston, Texas, USA. I still find it difficult to describe the deeply professional and personal impact that I have been honored to experience as I reflect upon my doctoral studies, tenure-track faculty years and as a tenured faculty member within the higher education university environment. Dr. Warner must be acknowledged as a true academic scholar and a true teacher educator.

Throughout my doctoral studies, Dr. Warner represented the faculty advisor guidance, patience, and benevolent oversight that developed my true understanding of the profession as one worthy of the highest esteem. Even after so many hours, days, months, and years of sacrificing his own time and effort toward supporting his students, the only request has been to *pass it forward* and impact others as profoundly as Dr. Warner impacted my own professional understanding and career path. I imagine that Dr. Warner may never know the true depth and breadth of his impact upon his students and colleagues, but I want to ensure this small acknowledgment highlights his truly significant career.

Finally, I would like to acknowledge the quality of university students with whom I have been honored to work. The undergraduate and graduate students with whom I have worked over the decades are exemplary examples of what I consider to be the best and the brightest within academia.

Students with whom I have been honored to work come from innumerable realms, including PreK-12 education systems as classroom teachers and professional staff, business and industry, medical education, higher education, and so many associated venues within which teaching, training, and instructional design quality support the vision and mission of the organizations. I learn just as much from my learner colleagues as what I share, and for this reinvigorating energy, creativity, innovation, and sense of community I am forever grateful.

Acknowledgments

SANDRA L. HARDY

The completion of the Commission on Classroom Teachers as Associated Teacher Educators three texts—*Redefining Teacher Preparation: Learning From Experience in Educator Development; Dynamic Principles of Professional Development: Essential Elements of Effective Teacher Preparation; Teacher to Teacher Mentality: Purposeful Practice in Teacher Education*—was made possible because of the diligent work ethic and dedication of so many individuals. I would like first and foremost to express immense gratitude to the Association of Teacher Educators (ATE) for bringing together a multitude of educators at all levels of the spectrum from preservice teachers through college deans.

ATE supports on so many levels the professional development of teachers, administrators, and teacher educators at all stages of their career and provides the opportunity to come together and learn from one another on a local, state, national, and international scale. ATE is also an organization that fosters teacher leadership. It is through the dynamic leadership and keen insight of former ATE president, Dr. Nancy P. Gallavan that our Commission on Classroom Teachers as Associated Teacher Educators came to fruition. Thank you, Dr. Nancy P. Gallavan.

Our commission was further enriched by the exemplary leadership of Dr. Caroline M. Crawford as commission chair. Dr. Crawford, also the coeditor of the afore mentioned books, time and again went far above and beyond the duties of chairing the commission to ensure that each member had ample opportunities to both express their ideas and unleash their full potential as commission members, members of the teaching profession and learning communities.

Further, Dr. Caroline M. Crawford served as an amazing mentor to me throughout the entire editing process. With Dr. Caroline M. Crawford's steadfast leadership, we rose time and again above and beyond tremendous challenges and recognized the importance of details to keep the texts moving forward. For all this and so much more, I am deeply thankful to Dr. Caroline. M. Crawford.

I pause at this juncture to recognize two outstanding teacher educators who influence and serve the education community in an exemplary fashion, Dr. D. John McIntyre and Dr. Christie McIntyre. Dr. D. John McIntyre, former ATE president, was also the chair of my doctoral committee as well as one of my teacher educators. Dr. D. John McIntyre serves as a shining example of an outstanding teacher educator, administrator, researcher, author, and editor. Dr. McIntyre provides encouragement and guidance to doctoral students and brings the long arduous journey of their dissertation to a successful defense.

Dr. Christie McIntyre, current ATE president for the Illinois State chapter, early childhood teacher educator, researcher, and role model for teacher educators, also contributes to doctoral students educational programs and committees, and serves the education communities in so many ways in her support to teachers, students, and as a model to teacher educators both in the university classroom and in the field as well as in to the learning communities. Thank you, Dr. D. John McIntyre and Dr. Christie McIntyre.

I would also like to express my sincere gratitude to each and every individual who contributed their work to the content of our commission's written works. Without their giving selflessly of their professional knowledge, skills, abilities, and time, the completion of these endeavors would not have been possible. Each author, as well as each assistant and associate reviewer, is a shining example of the education profession in their area of expertise. The culmination of these many individual professional teacher educators brought forth collectively the fruition of our Commission's efforts that will further serve to enrich the teaching profession and bring insight and support to many teachers across the teaching continuum for years to come. Thank you to all those teachers who made our mission a reality.

In closing, I embrace this opportunity to extend a heartfelt expression of gratitude to all of the truly dedicated professional educators who work tirelessly with compassion to make a difference in the life of so many individual teachers and learners in more ways than they may ever know. I further acknowledge with appreciation the multitude of learning communities who provide the support networks and link resources for teachers as learners and teacher educators to collaboratively improve their practice as they progress with renewal in all stages of professional development. Some of these educators participated in the completion of these texts, and some are a part of the research that is written about in the chapters.

Many are the educators who will find knowledge and support through the reading, discussion, and application of the content in the three texts brought forth by the Commission of Classroom Teachers as Associated Teacher Educators on behalf of the Association of Teacher Educators.

Editors' Note

Caroline M. Crawford and Sandra L. Hardy

The editors would like to thank the hard work and extensive efforts of their associate reviewers and assistant reviewers.

EDITORIAL ADVISORY BOARD OF REVIEWERS

Associate Reviewers: Book Chapter Manuscript Reviewers

The significant impact of the chapter associate reviewers was truly appreciated. Dr. Billi Bromer, Dr. Caroline M. Crawford, Dr. Nancy Gallavan, Dr. Sandra L. Hardy, and Dr. Jennifer Young extended their professional time expertise toward carefully reviewing and offering detailed feedback throughout the second round of book chapter double-blind reviews.

The editors would like to extend their heartfelt appreciation for these professionals who were able to extend themselves beyond the bounds of normal expectations of realistic quality and timeliness. Careful book chapter manuscript reviews were achieved within short time periods, and the detailed quality of support and engagement by each associate reviewer was impressive. For this, we, Dr. Crawford and Dr. Hardy, express our sincere appreciation.

Assistant Reviewers: Book Chapter Proposal Reviewers

The initial double-blind peer review efforts of the submitted proposals for the texts were extensions of professional creativity and innovation and were innumerable. The professional efforts and expertise of their assistant reviewers brought forward the strengths of each proposal, for which Dr. Crawford and Dr. Hardy would like to state their deep appreciation to: Dr. Billi Bromer, Dr. Lynda Cavazos, Dr. Caroline M. Crawford, Dr. Sandra L. Hardy, Dr. Lisa Huelskamp, and Dr. Nancy Gallavan.

They were integrally important, very much valued, respected, and each professional is highly esteemed for their depth of review effort. The high quality and impact of these scholarly works would not have been realized, without the assistant reviewer's initial strength of effort. For this, Dr. Crawford and Dr. Hardy offer significant thanks.

Introduction

Caroline M. Crawford and Sandra L. Hardy

ATE is a professional community focusing upon the dynamic principles of professional development as essential elements of effective teacher preparation. Dynamic principles of professional development are directly and indirectly defined and applied with no particular order of sequence as one or more of these principles may be activated in unison and revisited time and again in varied degrees and contexts throughout a professional's career. Further, this is by no means a list in the entirety of all professional principles pertaining to education, but rather a representation of the basis for the dynamic interchange that transpires and elevates professional development that is energized and authentic. These dynamic principles of professional development are as follows.

INTROSPECTION

Introspection is demonstrated in striving to improve and update knowledge and skills pertaining to professional practice of self and others. Introspection extends to courses, programs, and of those who teach or administer them in a type of internal communication of shared values, mutual objectives, and common purpose in promoting the professional development of improved practice that extends outward to support the educational profession.

PARTICIPATION

Participation as an active and continuing member of formal and informal support networks inclusive of but not limited to professional development organizations available to all novices at all stages of professional development which extends to more experienced teachers including administrators and other teacher educators to support and improve the educational profession.

COLLABORATION

Collaboration within and across multiple contexts with a broad range of colleagues to include local, national, and international frameworks that identify, locate, and distribute resources for professional development support and progression of the educational profession.

TRANSFORMATION

Transformation of the profession to increasingly improve singular and collective efforts to reach and connect meaningfully with greater numbers of teachers on all levels, stages of development, and situational circumstances to promote the professional development of the individual teacher and each learner they teach. Such transformation reaches across all contexts to involve individual teachers and learners through enriched reform evident in learning, learning to teach, and the essential elements of effective practice. Further this type of transformation transcends practical limitations of various variables such as budgetary constraints to inform research and practice that supports and improves the educational profession.

IDENTIFICATION

Identification of self as a professional within the educational profession presents a vantage point inclusive of the determination of professional development goals and objectives, as well as the identification of required resources and how to obtain them. Further within this dynamic principle is the identification of peers, for example, fellow novices and others as to their role and their professional development identification processes. The final outcome and purpose of these functioning dynamic principles is support and improvement of the educational profession.

The close association of each principle with the others is important to note as one informs the other. For example, "transformation of the profession" is the result of introspection, participation, and collaboration on multiple levels. Likewise, introspection is influenced by each of the other principles, and thus the close relationship of one upon the others is inseparable. These dynamic principles are inherent of the goals in the professional preparation and continue thereafter to improve the practice of classroom teachers as well as that of other educational professionals, including higher education faculty and administrators.

DYNAMIC PRINCIPLES OF PROFESSIONAL DEVELOPMENT AND THE CLASSROOM TEACHER AS ASSOCIATED TEACHER EDUCATOR

Further, these principles are often demonstrated in classroom teachers who also serve, often informally, as teacher educators or associated teacher educators. Therefore, a working definition is in order. A classroom teacher who takes on the role of an *associated teacher educator* is a quality professional, who focuses additional time, effort, and subject matter expertise upon supporting and training preservice teacher candidates, novice teachers, as well as experienced colleagues, and others within and across the field-based classroom environments.

Classroom teachers as associated teacher educators include, but are not limited to, a level of subject matter expertise; an understanding of the curricular design and student learner cognitive needs, instructional prowess within the current K-12 classroom experiential needs; dispositional understandings and the ability to assess the teacher candidates; support novices and more experienced educators across real-world settings; work with university teacher educators; and navigate and link the multitude of complex contextual and resource variations in the process.

Dynamic principles of professional development both illustrate and apply standards and dispositions evident within real-world classroom engagement, and while working closely with teachers, administrators, and university-based instructors. Classroom teachers as associated teacher educators routinely demonstrate the characteristics of these dynamic principles of professional development in their practice.

These principles often reflect elements of effective teacher preparation. Thus, these dynamic principles of professional development illuminate the key qualities of classroom teachers as associated teacher educators as well as enrich and expand the evolving definition of classroom teachers as associated teacher educators as the center focus of this text.

Therefore, this text is meant as a reflection of the current *state of the profession* as it revolves around the concept of classroom teachers as associated teacher educators. Further, this text serves also as a tool for promoting dynamic principles of professional development pertaining to professional discourse concerning the classroom teachers as associated teacher educators. This is such an important discussion to be had, and yet only recently has the teacher education profession more fully realized, acknowledged, and emphasized the integral impact of classroom teachers as associated teacher educators in this regard.

Such dynamic interchanges extend to teacher candidates, novice classroom teachers, and teacher educators. Further, these promote the continued excitement and innovative creativity necessary and appropriate for all of our classroom educators in order to attain and exhibit consistent displays of subject matter expertise, and an inherent understanding of the learning communities that integrates nuanced understandings associated with differentiated learning landscapes. These shared understandings and expertise as well as the ability to embrace lifelong learning coupled with resources serve to fuel the excitement of transformations found in professional renewal.

The enriched key points in the three texts highlight and integrate differences within the realm of teacher education through the theoretical, data-driven, and contextual realities of teaching and learning. These underpinnings are then the basis of the transformational journey toward becoming classroom teachers that also benefit veteran teachers in the process.

This framework is designated into three separate, yet related, books of focus:

- *Redefining Teacher Preparation: Learning From Experience in Educator Development*
- *Dynamic Principles of Professional Development: Essential Elements of Effective Teacher Preparation*
- *Teacher to Teacher Mentality: Purposeful Practice in Teacher Education*

Each text engages in intriguing frames of discussion from various regional areas of the United States of America. Further the chapters contained in each text explores the different types of school districts and parishes, including shifts from large metropolitan independent school districts and those pertaining to smaller towns and principalities that support and engage in teacher education field-based efforts.

One of the core strengths of the teacher education profession is the integral, continuous, and highly respected field-based classroom educators who formally and informally serve as associated teacher educators. Each of the texts extends and links the rich discourse beyond the bounds of the academic hallways into the teachers' classrooms, highlighting the amazing work efforts, professional dispositions of continuous engagement, nurturing efforts, and amazingly demonstrated professional kindness as displayed by classroom teachers in their roles as associated teacher educators working with university-based faculty.

The first text is titled *Redefining Teacher Preparation: Learning From Experience in Educator Development*. The chapters highlight applications and reflections of the Association of Teacher Educators (ATE) Standards for Teacher Educators and offer conceptual frameworks and contextual realities in connections to classroom educators at all stages of their career as associated teacher educators.

The transformational nature of the teacher education process reflected in these chapters reflects a deeper understanding of the professional shifts of theory and practice dynamics within and across school district as well as university-based teacher educators. These partnerships provide vast opportunities for professional development to learn and share through contextual engagement and communication of differentiated roles and associated experiential journeys that result in enriched practice and reflection as shared throughout the authored chapters.

The text *Dynamic Principles of Professional Development: Essential Elements of Effective Teacher Preparation* focuses upon differentiated elements toward inquiry and the reflectivity of practitioners as dynamic components of professional development. The chapters explore the sense of professional development that often occurs within the context of the field-based classroom experiences and school sites, while still allowing for a metaphoric dance that represents the deep connectivity linked to more formalized professional development opportunities.

Such opportunities include the sharing of experiences and engaging of useful instructional outcomes, as well as discourse that occurs among professional educators. These elements extend beyond the conceived ivory tower and are further integrated within the learning landscape of practice that is the pre-kindergarten through 12th-grade school districts and teachers' classrooms environmental venues.

Hence, the chapters in this text illustrate classroom teachers as associated teacher educators engaged in powerful and effective mentorships and collegial support networks within and across contexts of learning and learning how to teach. These integral processes are further intricately interconnected within multiple levels of influence and engagement that reflectively results in a continuing dialogue of understanding and impact that connects learning communities to improve practice as evidenced in the authored chapters.

The text *Teacher to Teacher Mentality: Purposeful Practice in Teacher Education* focuses upon professional discourse that revolves around induction efforts and highlights dispositional understandings associated with effective teacher leaders. These elements as well as teacher candidate collegial support by classroom teachers are also explored in the chapters.

These key concepts integrate and form the basis of effective collaborations between teacher candidates, classroom teachers, field-based university supervisors, and teacher education faculty that resonate in the chapters. An intriguing shift within this text are the dispositional underpinnings as framed through communities of learning, communities of practice (Wenger, 1998, 2009) as well as Wenger's more recent learning in landscapes of practice (Wenger-Trayner, Fenton-O'Creevy, Hutchinson, Kubiak, & Wenger-Trayner, 2015).

This text is offered to serve as a guiding framework that is adjustable as a useful tool toward developing and transforming pathways in meeting the professional development needs of the individual classroom teacher as associated teacher educators. It is important to emphasize that this framework has moveable components and therefore shifts to suit various contexts and levels of teacher development, including those paradigms of teacher educators at the university and beyond.

The following chapters further reflect the development of an approach toward professional understanding and professionalism of teacher educators within and across all levels and contexts of teacher education discourse and engagement.

REFERENCES

Wenger, E. (1998). *Communities of practice: Learning, meaning, and identity*. Cambridge, MA: Harvard University Press.

Wenger, E. (2009). A social theory of learning. In K. Illeris (Ed.), *Contemporary theories of learning: Learning theorists . . . in their own words*. New York, NY: Routledge.

Wenger-Trayner, E., Fenton-O'Creevy, M., Hutchinson, S., Kubiak, C., & Wenger-Trayner, B. (2015). *Learning in landscapes of practice: Boundaries, identify, and knowledgeability in practice-based learning*. New York, NY: Routledge.

Overview and Framework
Caroline M. Crawford and Sandra L. Hardy

This text is offered to serve as a guiding framework that is adjustable as a useful tool toward developing and transforming pathways in applying the dynamic principles of professional development pertaining to needs of the individual classroom teacher with special emphasis on classroom teachers as associated teacher educators. It is important to emphasize that this framework has moveable and malleable components and therefore purposefully shifts to suit various contexts and levels of teacher development, including those paradigms of teacher educators at the university.

The following chapters further reflect the development of an approach toward professional understanding and professionalism of teacher educators within and across all levels and contexts of teacher and teacher educator preparation.

Dynamic Principles of Professional Development: Essential Elements of Effective Teacher Preparation reflects differentiated inquiry and reflectivity as a fluctuating yet constant connection to educational practitioners as individuals and collectively as functional members of the professional education communities.

The chapters that follow explore the sense of professional development that often occurs within the context of the field-based classroom experiences and school sites, while still allowing for a metaphoric dance between more formalized professional development opportunities. Such opportunities include the sharing of experiences and engaging useful instructional outcomes, as well as dialogue for teachers, administrators, and teacher educators at all levels and stages of preparation and development.

The text centers around professional development and teacher preparation as interlinked and important aspects of educational understanding that affect change and therefore serve as potentials for reform (Hargreaves, Lieberman,

Fullan, & Hopkins, 1998; 2009). It is clear within the Information Age that educational change is a ubiquitous experience that has held prominence within national conversations and brought forward laws, policies, and monetary allocations that are utterly amazing due to the sheer and often overwhelming nature of transformation involved in paradigm shifts.

Yet this is a macro view of professional development and teacher preparation that is both derived from within and transcends the field of teacher education with repercussions and ramifications upon classroom teachers. A micro view is also a vitally important discussion reflecting upon the impact of professional development and teacher preparation within a snapshot of the teacher education profession (Bates, Swennen, & Jones, 2011; de Lima Ferreira & Bertotti, 2016; Gibbons & Knapp, 2015; Stewart, 2014).

The intriguing dichotomy between the realms of professional development and professional discourse is the recognition that developmental activities and dialogue don't always intersect with teacher preparation. There is a growing discussion stemming from an emphasis upon engagement and engaging in a community that communicates (Dankoski, Brown, & Gusic, 2015; Gibbons & Knapp, 2015).

Attempts over the years have focused upon engaging in professional development schools, focusing upon not only a field-based teacher education approach but also the conception that the school site embraces learning as a transformational engagement by the classroom students, as well as teacher candidates, classroom teachers, field-based supervisors, and university faculty. A holistic learning landscape approach toward professional development and collegial dialogue may embrace Wenger's learning in a landscape of practice approach (Wenger, 1998, 2009; Wenger-Trayner, Fenton-O'Creevy, Hutchinson, Kubiak, & Wenger-Trayner, 2015), further engaging an intriguing discussion revolving around professional development and discourse.

The chapters in this text illustrate dynamic principles of professional development evident in the practice of classroom teachers as associated teacher educators engaged in powerful and effective mentorships and collegial support networks. These processes are further enhanced within multiple levels of impact and engagement that reflectively result in a continuing dialogue of understanding that connects learning communities to improve teacher preparation and practice as evidenced in the authored chapters.

Pylman, Stanulis, and Wexler focus their discussion in chapter 1, "Mentors as Associated Teacher Educators: Inquiry as Professional Development," upon an inquiry professional development approach as encompassed by mentors with teacher candidates. From a reflective approach toward practice, the authors take part in a discussion wherein mentors are supported through professional development participation that evolves the Socratic method of questioning and discussion toward a level of analytic inquiry.

The authors transform the study of inquiry as professional development into a resulting professional development model that embraces effective inquiry by mentor teachers so as to impact teacher candidates through a shift from traditional mentoring toward educative mentoring understanding and implementation.

Hardy brings forward chapter 2, "Transforming Induction: Contexts and Practice," with an insightful site-based understanding of induction program development tailored to suit each school and teacher in mentoring educators from the perspective of novice and new to the district teachers. The author draws from a strong theoretical undergirding while emphasizing qualitative data sets that tell an insightful story of the need toward transforming induction, contexts, and practice throughout the professional education realm.

In chapter 3, "Teachers Learning Together at Auburn Elementary: Supporting Classroom Teachers as Associated Teacher Educators," Carver, Hudson, Abbott, Bruha, Bugaj, Johnson, and Stock framed a discussion around teachers learning together within an elementary school setting, specifically as framed through the engagement of clinical-based teacher preparation efforts. Clinical practice is at the heart of this discussion, focusing upon schools that embrace the learning in a landscape of practice approach (Wenger, 1998, 2009; Wenger-Trayner et al., 2015).

Classroom teachers as associated teacher educators are supported through professional learning opportunities that are carefully crafted and focus upon rich opportunities that not only enhance engagement by classroom teachers but also enrich the associated teacher educator work with teacher candidates.

In chapter 4, "Promoting ATE Standard for Professional Development in Pre-K Settings," Moffett, Frizzell, Brownlee-Williams, Blount, and Moffett bring forward an intriguing discussion that evolves a pre-kindergarten classroom teacher case study–based action research effort into a focused approach toward the growth of classroom teachers. Results of the case study methodology reflect understandings related to the needs associated with classroom management, professional development within a small group and lesson implementation efforts with developed sensitivity toward cultural and socio-economic diversity.

One may suggest that the study's findings reflect the professionalism of classroom teachers as associated teacher educators, who continue to engage in areas of growth in these arenas of continuous focus found in the teacher education field.

Finally, in chapter 5, "Teacher Educators as Collegial Mentors: Integrating Instructional Technologies Through an Extended Community of Practice

Professional Development Approach," Crawford brings forward an instrumental multiple case study approach (Stake, 2005) that implements personal documents and personal communications within a grounded theory analytic approach (Charmaz, 2014; Creswell, 2007) toward realizing the thematic results.

Graduate students who were also classroom teachers and collegial mentors self-selected to engage in an instructional technology course that embraced Digital Age social engagement tools as well as production-focused instructional products toward impacting their instructional and curricular efforts. Designated themes that arose were five: self-efficacy, collegiality, creativity, knowledge base, and professional impact.

The recognition of the course experiences resulted in thematic implications that suggested an evolving self-efficacy of teacher educators as collegial mentors, while also emphasizing thematic realities of support within and across learning landscapes of practice (Wenger, 1998, 2009; Wenger-Trayner et al., 2015).

REFERENCES

Bates, T., Swennen, A., & Jones, K. (2011). *The professional development of teacher educators*. London: Routledge. Retrieved from https://core.ac.uk/download/files/333/11046799.pdf

Charmaz, K. (2014). *Constructing grounded theory*. Thousand Oaks, CA: SAGE Publications Ltd.

Creswell, J. W. (2007). *Qualitative inquiry and research design: Choosing among five traditions* (2nd ed.). Thousand Oaks, CA: Sage Publications.

Dankoski, M., Brown, A., & Gusic, M. (2015). Peer coaching to counteract organizational silence and foster a culture of dialogue. *MedEdPORTAL Publications, 11*, 10133.

de Lima Ferreira, J., & Bertotti, G. R. (2016). Continuing education for professional development in higher education teaching. *Creative Education, 7*(10), 1425–1435. Retrieved from http://file.scirp.org/pdf/CE_2016071216471636.pdf

Gibbons, L., & Knapp, M. (2015). Talk that teaches: How to promote professional dialogue and growth. *Journal of Staff Development, 36*(3), 14.

Hargreaves, A., Lieberman, A., Fullan, M., Hopkins, D. W. (Eds.). (1998). *International Handbook of Educational Change: Part Two*. Netherlands, Springer Netherlands. doi: 10.1007/978-94-011-4944-0

Hargreaves, A., Lieberman, A., Fullan, M., Hopkins, D. W. (Eds.). (2009). *Second International Handbook of Educational Change*. Netherlands, Springer Netherlands. doi: 10.1007/978-90-481-2660-6

Stake, R. E. (2005). Qualitative case studies. In N. K. Denzin & Y. S. Lincoln (Eds.), *The Sage handbook of qualitative research* (3rd ed., pp. 443–466). Thousand Oaks, CA: Sage.

Stewart, C. (2014). Transforming professional development to professional learning. *Journal of Adult Education, 43*(1), 28. Retrieved from http://files.eric.ed.gov/fulltext/EJ1047338.pdf

Wenger, E. (1998). *Communities of practice: Learning, meaning, and identity*. Cambridge, MA: Harvard University Press.

Wenger, E. (2009). A social theory of learning. In K. Illeris (Ed.), *Contemporary theories of learning: Learning theorists . . . in their own words*. New York, NY: Routledge.

Wenger-Trayner, E., Fenton-O'Creevy, M., Hutchinson, S., Kubiak, C., & Wenger-Trayner, B. (2015). *Learning in landscapes of practice: Boundaries, identify, and knowledgeability in practice-based learning*. New York, NY: Routledge.

Chapter 1

Mentors as Associated Teacher Educators: Inquiry as Professional Development

Stacey Pylman, Randi Stanulis, and
Lindsay Joseph Wexler

ABSTRACT

Mentor teachers are integral to teacher education but are rarely prepared to inquire about the impact of their work on beginning teacher development. This chapter describes mentor professional development that is targeted and supports mentors in this teacher educator role. This professional development model has been both enacted and studied in several large urban contexts. First, examples of traditional mentoring in action are provided, as contrasted with a view of educative mentoring focused on beginning teacher learning goals. Second, a vision of mentoring that embodies principles of mentors as teacher educators is defined. Third, core mentoring practices that provide the focus of the professional development are detailed. Lastly, the possibilities of a teacher leader development, based on inquiry, are presented.

KEYWORDS

Beginning teacher, educative mentoring, mentoring, novice teacher, professional development, student teaching, teacher education, traditional Mentoring

In order to improve education, beginning teachers need better educational opportunities while learning to teach in the classroom context. Mentor teachers (classroom teachers who mentor beginning or student teachers) are integral to teacher education but are rarely prepared to inquire about the impact of their work on beginning teacher development. It is common to assume that if a teacher is considered an effective teacher, the teacher is also an effective mentor. A mentor may be an expert classroom teacher, but that does not necessarily mean the mentor knows how to be a teacher educator—one who is able to educate the beginning teacher (Gareis & Grant, 2014; Schwille, 2008; Timperley, 2001).

Mentors need to be reflective and analytical with their own teaching practice and guide the beginning teacher to do the same. Mentors need to make their instructional decision making explicit for the beginning teachers. They need to identify specific beginning teacher learning goals and use mentoring practices in an intentional way to help beginning teachers reach those goals. Mentors have the potential to make a significant contribution in helping a beginning teacher learn to be an effective teacher who makes a difference in student learning, if adequately supported and prepared with a teacher educator goal in mind.

COMPARING EDUCATIVE TO TRADITIONAL MENTORING

Traditionally, mentoring is viewed as giving support to the beginning teacher to lessen the stress of learning to teach (Bradbury, 2010; Little, 1990). The role of the mentor is also viewed as someone who will open up his or her classroom and allow the beginning teacher a place to practice while the mentor provides practical support, advice, and teaching strategies based on immediate needs (Bradbury, 2010; Leatham & Peterson, 2010).

A traditional mentoring approach also includes sharing practical solutions to day-to-day problems and providing resources (Bradbury, 2010). Although traditional mentoring helps to retain beginning teachers and lessen their stress as they learn a new career, research by Feiman-Nemser (2001) and Norman and Feiman-Nemser (2005) increased our understanding of the role of mentors as teacher educators.

If mentors are really teacher educators, mentoring practice should build from simply providing emotional and technical support. Instead, mentors need to view themselves as "educative mentors," a term coined by Feiman-Nemser (1998) to describe mentoring as a way to meet the immediate needs of the beginning teacher while also focusing on long-term goals for growth toward reform-based teaching (Bell, Stanulis, & Macaluso, 2016; Feiman-Nemser, 2001; Norman & Feiman-Nemser, 2005).

> Educative mentoring rests on an explicit vision of good teaching and an understanding of teacher learning. Mentors who share this orientation attend to beginning teachers' present concerns, questions, and purposes without losing sight of long-term goals for teacher development. They interact with beginning teachers in ways that foster an inquiring stance. They cultivate skills and habits that enable beginning teachers to learn in and from their practice. They use their knowledge and expertise to assess the direction novices are heading and to create opportunities and conditions that support meaningful teacher learning in the service of student learning. (Feiman-Nemser, 2001, p. 18)

According to Bradbury (2010) and Feiman-Nemser (2001) core principles of educative mentoring include learning through inquiry into teaching practice, focusing attention on student thinking and understanding, co-thinking and decision making around problems of practice, valuing the contributions and ideas of both the mentor and the beginning teacher, and intentionally aligning mentoring practice with beginning teacher learning goals (Pylman, 2016).

Scholars agree that educative mentoring is effective in guiding beginning teacher growth toward reformed-based teaching practices. Schwille (2008) believes that educative mentoring helps beginning teachers learn the disposition to learn in and from their practice. Bradbury (2010) argued that educative mentoring led beginning teachers to grow in reformed-based science teaching. Stanulis and Brondyk (2013) found that educative mentoring helped beginning teachers learn and apply discussion-based teaching methods. In an empirical study, Stanulis, Little, and Wibbens (2012) found that beginning teachers who were supported with targeted mentoring that promoted a shared vision of good teaching improved in their teaching effectiveness compared to beginning teachers in the same district who did not receive this targeted mentoring.

MENTORING WITH BEGINNING TEACHER LEARNING GOALS IN MIND

Intentional mentors who use educative mentoring to help beginning teachers reach learning goals need to be able to articulate what they are mentoring toward (Stanulis, Brondyk, Little, & Wibbens, 2014). The central questions for educative mentoring should be, *What do beginning teachers need to learn? And, how do we help them reach these learning goals to improve pupil learning?*

Beginning teachers need to learn how to gather and analyze student data to focus on student learning. The purpose of teaching is for students to learn. Most often beginning teachers are so wrapped up in their performance as teachers and the execution of their plans that they forget the point of their lesson is student learning (Pitton, 2006). How do mentors help interns focus on student learning objectives? Mentoring practice should focus on helping the beginning teacher plan and reflect based on student learning objectives, while also giving feedback to the beginning teacher that uses student thinking and work as data (or evidence of learning) for analysis (Hiebert, Morris, Berk, & Jansen, 2007).

Beginning teachers have differentiated learning needs. Mentors need to understand the learning progression of a particular beginning teacher and ways to scaffold learning to assist performance (Wang & Paine, 2001). Mentoring practice should consider specific learning opportunities a beginning teacher may need, provide content-specific assistance or clarification, and consider how to incorporate the beginning teacher's vision of effective teaching.

PROFESSIONAL DEVELOPMENT FOR MENTOR TEACHERS

Schwille (2008) concluded, "Much like teaching, [educative] mentoring that is aimed at helping novices learn to teach is a professional practice with a repertoire of skill sets that must be learned over time" (p. 139). If mentor teachers are to enact their role as teacher educators, a certain kind of professional development (PD) needs to occur to provide targeted support to mentors in enacting educative practices.

In order to help mentor teachers understand their role as teacher educators, it is important for PD designers to understand what it means to be a teacher educator and the benefits of enacting such a role, take into account evidence of effective PD, consider who should provide the PD, and define the core mentoring practices in an elaborative manner.

Role as a Teacher Educator

Mentor teachers are teacher educators, but they often do not recognize this aspect of their role or receive adequate preparation and support to be fully effective (Feiman-Nemser, 1998; Feiman-Nemser & Buchmann, 1987). Mentors work with beginning teachers to help them grow in independence as they teach and make instructional decisions. The mentor is a school-based teacher educator, who joins the beginning teacher in "inquiry about teaching and learning to teach" (Feiman-Nemser, 1998, p. 66).

A mentor teacher's role can extend far beyond providing emotional support and helping to put out fires; as a teacher educator, the mentor teacher's primary goal is to help the beginning teacher to expand his or her vision of teaching to individual student learning. Through modeling, thinking aloud, asking critical questions, reflecting, listening to the beginning teacher, and working on inquiry tasks together, mentor teachers fully embody the role of a teacher educator (Feiman-Nemser, 1998).

Benefits

When supported in practice and prepared for their role, mentor teachers provide considerable benefits to the school, students, university, and beginning teacher. Just as the job of teaching can be considered isolating (Lortie, 1975), being a mentor teacher, too, is often isolating (Bell, 2015). Shared learning and teaching expertise in communities reduces mentor teacher isolation (Borko, 2004; Warren-Little, 2006; Warren-Little, Gearhart, Curry, & Kafka, 2003). In such a professional community, mentor teachers can take part in PD that provides an opportunity for reflection on practices as a mentor as well as a classroom teacher (Schon, 1983).

This contributes to the learning of the students in the classroom as well as the learning and growth of the beginning teacher. PD for mentor teachers has the ability to support mentors in developing educative practices. The core practices of co-planning, observing and debriefing, and analyzing student work can focus the mentoring practice on student learning, thus benefiting the beginning teacher in addition to the students in the classroom (Stanulis, Pylman, & Wexler, 2015).

Effective Professional Development

The importance of PD for mentor teachers cannot be denied, but what is the best way to educate and provide PD for mentor teachers? The outcomes of PD are defined by Feiman-Nemser (2001) as a transformation in the knowledge, understanding, skills, and/or commitments in the teacher (Feiman-Nemser, 2001). One-time PD is not sufficient to help mentors understand educative mentoring practices, allow for practice and reflection, and provide space for inquiry learning in collaboration with others. Bullough (2009), Desimone (2009), and DuFour (2004) believe that effective PD contains certain criteria. In Table 1.1 effective PD is paralleled with the benefits of mentor PD.

According to DuFour (2004) the main tenets of PD communities include a focus on learning rather than teaching, members working collaboratively, members examining student work and thinking through data analysis, and teachers being held accountable for results. The proposed PD structure in this

Table 1.1. Effective Mentor Professional Development

Criteria of Effective Professional Development (Bullough, 2009; Desimone, 2009; DuFour, 2004)	Proposed Mentor Professional Development
Content focus and inquiry-based	Inquiry into beginning teacher learning, effective teaching practice, and educative mentoring practice
Active learning	Discussion and immediate application of learning to mentoring practice (trying it out)
Coherence	Mentors apply learning to a specific context (their classroom) and beginning teacher learning needs
Duration	Monthly meetings are sustained over the academic year
Collective participation	Attended by mentors in the same school or district
Collaboration	Mentors share practice, ideas, experience, learning, and feedback

chapter provides mentor teachers an opportunity to discuss and analyze each other's practice with the purpose of shared learning through inquiry. Many teachers who participate in PD with other mentor teachers benefit not only from their own participation, but from the participation and collaboration (collegial inquiry) of their colleagues as well (Drago-Severson, 2007; Hobson, Ashby, Malderez, & Tomlinson, 2009; Warren-Little, 2006; Warren-Little et al., 2003).

MENTORING AS AN INQUIRY PROCESS

A reflective practitioner who inquiries into practice is more likely to grow and develop as a teacher (Schon, 1983). The proposed mentor PD in this chapter leads mentors to inquire into beginning teacher learning, student learning (in cooperation with the beginning teacher), teaching, and mentoring practice.

One of the central questions of mentoring practice is, what do beginning teachers need to learn? By inquiring into beginning teacher learning goals during mentor PD, mentors are able to apply their learning of mentoring practice in a specific context of intern needs. Mentors are able to focus their co-planning, observations, and feedback on specific intern learning goals. A focus on intern learning goals is a tenant of educative mentoring.

Inquiry into student learning is an effective way to analyze and inquire into teaching practice (Heibert et al., 2007). As mentors guide beginning teachers to inquire into student learning, both mentor and beginning teacher are able to learn about their teaching practice. Mentoring practice should focus on helping the beginning teacher plan and reflect based on student learning objectives, while also giving feedback to the beginning teacher that uses student thinking and work as data (or evidence of learning) for analysis (Hiebert et al., 2007).

Lastly, as mentors engage in PD they will inquire into their own mentoring practice. The second central question guiding mentoring practice (after answering *what do beginning teachers need to learn?)* is, how do we help beginning teachers reach these learning goals together to improve pupil learning?

The latter question is answered through enactment of educative mentoring practices that promote inquiry around teacher and student learning. Inquiring into mentoring practice helps mentors identify the mentoring practices they are currently using, and opens themselves to developing more educative practices to help beginning teachers reach learning goals.

Professional Development Content

Across the mentoring literature and current PD practice, there are three commonly held practices effective mentor teachers can enact to guide beginning teachers to be successful, independent teachers. These practices include co-planning, observing and debriefing, and engaging in student work analysis.

However, there are traditional and educative ways for mentors to enact these mentoring practices. PD for mentor teachers can help mentors grow in their ability to move from traditional mentoring to a more educative mentoring approach. First each practice is described, and illustrations of educative practice are provided. Then an explanation is given for how the mentoring practices should be learned and enacted through mentor PD.

Co-planning. Co-planning can provide an educational setting for both mentor and beginning teachers. However, not all co-planning sessions are educative. It is commonplace for mentors to engage in "scheduling" where they spend some time sitting down with the calendar and talking through what will be done throughout the week. Typically, mentors will share what they do and beginning teachers usually choose to mimic. This practice can be supportive, but it is not educative in helping beginning teachers learn how to teach and make instructional decisions independently.

For a co-planning session to be educative, mentors need to make their thinking and decision making transparent as they model for the beginning teacher (Pylman, 2016). This means mentors need to explain why they make certain instructional choices based on standards, objectives, student need, or curricular requirements. Mentors need to be prepared and intentional about the conversations they will have during co-planning sessions. They should go into co-planning thinking about possible teachable moments during the session.

For example, mentors may choose to explore and clarify content, discuss curriculum or standard requirements, or explicitly teach how to use student data to inform instruction. Lastly, the mentor should also encourage the beginning teacher to explain his or her thinking and decision making (Pylman, in press).

Mentors are extremely busy as they juggle the demands of the classroom and the demands of mentoring. Why should mentors take the extra time to co-plan with their beginning teachers? Remember, the goal of educative mentoring is to prepare the beginning teachers so they are able to make instructional decisions independently once they leave the mentor's classroom. Unless the mentor takes time to model co-planning, decision making, and thought processes, the beginning teacher will be on his or her own to learn how to effectively plan.

Specifically, a beginning teacher needs to learn what is necessary to think about when planning and how student learning is central in the planning process. While planning for co-planning sessions, mentors should consider the following questions: What does a beginning teacher need to learn about planning? How will co-planning with me make this teacher a better teacher? Do I want my intern to be able to teach a lesson I've taught before *OR* be prepared to teach a lesson in response to student need, curriculum, standards, context so when he or she leaves, he or she can create his or her own lessons and units? What does educative co-planning look like when mentors intentionally prepare to teach beginning teachers during sessions?

Mentors and beginning teachers explore content together (Feiman-Nemser & Beasley, 1997). Exploring content can include explaining confusing concepts, articulating the understanding of the content, looking at definitions, pre-warning the intern about what may be confusing for students. In educative co-planning sessions mentors explain instructional decisions they make based on standards, objectives, student need, or curricula requirements.

Even though the beginning teacher might not ask, mentors answer questions such as, why do I teach this in this particular way? How do I approach this content? Where do I expect misconceptions to occur? Where might students need extra support? How will I assess the success of this lesson?

It is essential that mentors also maintain a focus on student learning, through reference to student data and asking the following questions: What do we know about our students? What do they already know? What do we want students to learn? How will we get them there? How will we know they got there? Lastly, mentors need to leave space for the beginning teacher to ask questions as they model their planning and thinking—until the beginning teacher takes on more planning responsibility at which time the mentor explains less and asks more questions of the beginning teacher to elicit his or her thinking (Pylman, in press).

Observation and debrief. Observing and debriefing are common mentoring activities but need careful enactment in order to be educative. For an observation to be educative, mentors need to focus on an area of instructional consequence (Stanulis & Bell, 2016). This can be accomplished by selecting a focused purpose for the observation related to an area of teaching effectiveness, such as questioning, student understanding, using formative assessment, or student engagement. With this targeted purpose in mind, the mentor can then collect data consistent with the selected purpose.

Examples of evidence a mentor can collect include counting the number of times certain students talk, providing specific examples of teacher questions asked throughout a lesson, scripting specific comments from students who don't understand an idea, noting specifics about behaviors of students who are not engaged, and providing the timing of each lesson component in order to analyze the use of instructional time.

A mentor should not collect too much data, or the beginning teacher will be overwhelmed. Mentors need to use the data to support a specific claim about the focal point of the inquiry. If a mentor provides a laundry list of everything that needs to be "fixed" at once, rather than target a small focus area to improve, the beginning teacher can become overwhelmed and dismiss the mentoring. Observations provide a site for inquiry in support of teacher learning where teachers can learn in and from their teaching practice in collaboration with a mentor (Ball & Cohen, 1999; Stanulis & Ames, 2009).

In a study of one mentor who was developing her own educative mentoring practice, she described the ways she now approaches her mentoring. Educative mentoring to this teacher, Debbie, included: (a) Learning to observe by looking for evidence; (b) Learning to hold critical conversations about teaching; (c) Learning to confront difficult situations in order to move a beginning teacher's practice forward, and (d) Learning to help beginning teachers find their own unique voice and principled reasons for teaching decisions (Stanulis & Ames, 2009). The theme of these findings is that having focused, evidence-based conversations based on observational data helped this mentor be educative.

The enactment of the conversation or debriefing that follows an observation must be carefully planned. For a debriefing to be educative, mentors need to: (a) have a clear focus and purpose that can be growth producing; (b) plan verbally and nonverbally to have a clear opening moment that sets the tone for the conversation (posture, facial expressions, beginning words, showing interest and enthusiasm in the intern's learning); (c) use appropriate data from the observation to help a beginning teacher target improvement; (d) ask questions to elicit intern thinking rather than "telling"; and (e) reinforce strong practices seen (Stanulis & Brondyk, 2014). With careful planning and practice, this approach to debriefing can be internalized and provide for fruitful, instructional conversations to occur.

Student work analysis. The primary goal of mentor teachers is to provide beginning teachers with experiences that grow their vision of teaching from simply focusing on their teaching performance to focus more on the learning of the individual students in the classroom (Pitton, 2006). Using student knowledge and needs to drive instruction is important for helping beginning teachers develop their vision of teaching.

The practice of analyzing student work provides teachers with timely evidence of students' understanding, which influences future instructional decisions and allows the teacher to reflect on prior instruction. For the beginning teacher, the modeling and thinking aloud done by the mentor teacher during this process allows for an educative learning experience. Analyzing student work prepares beginning teachers to learn *from* teaching.

To begin the student work analysis process, the mentor or beginning teacher selects a task/assignment for analysis. This can be any assessing artifact from a lesson, either formative or summative. The mentor and beginning teacher discuss the student learning targets/objectives from the lesson and determine the expectations for the task/assignment ("Standards-based protocol for analyzing student work," n.d.).

Next, they define what it means to meet expectations, to exceed expectations, or to not meet expectations. Together they analyze student work and sort it into piles according to progress toward objectives. It is important they discuss the quality of the work and explain justification for sorting decisions (Yusko & Feiman-Nemser, 2008). While it is important to have an understanding of student work collectively, for the beginning teacher it is especially important to focus on a few students' papers to analyze their work in depth and think about ways to differentiate instruction to meet the individual learning needs.

Based on the amount of time available, the mentor and beginning teacher select a student sample from each of the three piles. They identify what the student does understand, is struggling to understand, what the student needs next, and create a plan to help the student reach the learning objectives ("Standards-based protocol for analyzing student work," n.d.). Finally, the mentor and beginning teacher reflect on how the instruction influenced student learning. They consider teacher moves made, explicitness of instructions, and take into account the various factors that may have influenced student learning.

In order for student work analysis to be an educative experience, the mentor teacher must think aloud while considering how the student work aligns to the learning objectives and explain the reasoning for decisions made. After student work has been sorted, the educative mentor reflects with the beginning teacher on the alignment between student work, learning objectives, and the instruction of the lesson.

It is important they identify the learning needs of specific individuals that became evident during the student work analysis process. The educative mentor will create a plan with the beginning teacher to target the students whose learning needs may not have been met. This practice provides an opportunity for educators to scaffold and differentiate learning opportunities based upon students' learning needs and strengths that emerge during the work analysis. The educative practice of analyzing student work influences future planning and instruction; thus, it is important to conclude the discussion with a conversation about how future instruction will look different because of the analysis.

PROFESSIONAL DEVELOPMENT STRUCTURE

We, the authors, propose that each mentor PD session focus primarily on one of these three core mentoring practices. To guide the mentors in the educative mentoring practice, PD sessions will facilitate learning through focused inquiry into beginning teacher learning. In the session, mentors learn about one educative mentoring practice through examples, discussion, and video.

Following the session, mentors apply their learning to their own mentoring practice and afterward reflect on the implementation as it relates to both student and beginning teacher learning. In subsequent PD sessions, mentors share success and collaborate with other mentors to problem solve and critically think about the learning opportunities created through the enactment of the educative mentoring practices. In this manner the learning is not static but is applied into practice and analyzed further.

WHO SHOULD PROVIDE MENTOR PROFESSIONAL DEVELOPMENT?

All mentor teachers can benefit from participation in inquiry-based, data-driven, sustained PD, but who should be responsible for providing it? Teacher preparation programs benefit from fostering a positive and productive mentor-beginning teacher collaborative relationship where beginning teachers are involved in learning more about the day-to-day experiences of classroom teachers and school contexts.

As a result, some might argue the teacher preparation program should lead the mentor PD. However, schools also benefit from the collaboration between mentor and beginning teachers.

School district mentors who mentor first- or second-year teachers also benefit from sustained participation in mentor PD (Stanulis et al., 2012). Those who mentor grow as professionals in leadership capacity, analytical reflection on teaching, and subsequent teaching practice (Brondyk & Stanulis, 2014; Stanulis, Cooper, Dear, Johnson, & Todd, 2016). Mentees have the potential to grow as effective, analytical teachers with quality mentoring and have an impact on student learning early in their career.

Teacher preparation programs that provide PD for both university mentors and school-based mentors can stimulate a mutual benefit relationship between universities and schools. Because both parties gain from the growth and development of mentor teachers, we argue teacher preparation programs and school districts collaborate on providing mentor PD. Although all parties benefit, it will be the students of the beginning teachers who will benefit the most.

DEVELOPING TEACHER LEADERS

Through participation in PD, mentor teachers will develop leadership strategies that will benefit the schools in which they work. The analytical practices mentors develop for working with beginning teachers also extend to their own teaching practice. When inquiring about student learning with beginning teachers, the mentor teachers look at their own teaching in different ways to explain *why* they make the decisions they do.

A mentor viewing his or her role as a teacher educator purposefully collects data to help the beginning teacher think about his or her teaching; develops data collection and analysis skills benefiting the beginning teacher and the mentor himself or himself. Mentoring practices influence teaching practices. Seeing the mentor role as a teacher educator influences the mentor's identity. Identifying as a teacher educator helps mentors develop as teacher leaders. Spending time reflecting on teaching practices helps mentors strengthen their instruction, as well as develop a knowledge base that can be shared with beginning teachers and other veteran teachers.

Schools must create conditions for learning so that teacher leaders have voice and agency in developing their mentor roles (Lieberman, 2015); this is important to encourage educative practices and teacher leadership. Schools need to foster what Fairman and Mackenzie (2015) call a "collegial climate," important in encouraging teacher leadership (p. 72).

When teachers value their colleagues and respect their pedagogical practices, schools become open to an environment in which teacher leaders can be very influential in encouraging learning, taking risks, and valuing collaboration. If schools are to grow and improve, teachers need to play a role in influencing the kind of teaching that develops in the school. Inquiry through mentoring can help with this process (Cooper et al., 2015).

Educative mentor teachers are continual learners, always striving to improve their practice. When engaged in mentoring PD, teachers acquire reflective strategies that can improve the teaching practices of beginning teachers as well as their own teaching practice. With the desire to better understand *why*, mentor teachers see the importance in questioning their own practice.

By using analytical practices, mentors look at their own teaching in different ways. An educative mentor possesses traits of a quality teacher. After all, "The tools of mentoring—observation, co-planning, co-teaching, joint inquiry, critical conversation and reflection—are also the tools of continuous improvement in teaching" (Feiman-Nemser, 1998, p. 73).

When teachers value the ongoing process of learning as a teacher and participate in mentor PD, they develop data collection and analysis skills to improve instructional practice. As someone who continually strives for new knowledge, teacher educators are likely to seek outside or additional opportunities for learning. Sharing at conferences, reading scholarly and practitioner literature, attending and leading PD are all ways the teacher educator becomes a teacher leader.

Teacher leaders influence the culture in the school; their mind-set of inquiry as a way of being can benefit the school community (Brondyk & Stanulis, 2014). By sharing their practices, mentors can influence change. As York-Barr and Duke (2004) explain,

> Teacher expertise is at the foundation of increasing teacher quality . . . this expertise becomes more widely available when accomplished teachers model effective instruction practices, encourage sharing of best practices, mentor new teachers, and collaborate with teaching colleagues. (pp. 258–259)

By participating in PD as a mentor, educative teachers collaborate with their colleagues, model and share practices, and work with beginning teachers, benefiting the students and teachers within the entire school community.

CONCLUSION

A well-designed and sustained mentor PD is necessary to support mentor teachers developing educative mentoring roles. The core mentoring practices of co-planning, observing and debriefing, and analyzing student work are central to educating teachers who will become independent instructional decision makers considering all their learners.

Using inquiry to concentrate efforts on student learning, this model for mentoring PD uses mentoring practice to help the beginning teacher's vision of teaching expand to focus on individual student learning. Involving mentors as educational partners in learning to teach is essential in improving teacher education.

The Association of Teacher Education professional standards highlight high-quality professional development, collaboration, and teaching as critical components in efforts to elevate the teaching profession. This effort to prepare mentors as teacher educators can be pivotal in bridging the university-school divide and escalating the role of teachers as leaders.

REFERENCES

Ball, D. L. & Cohen, D. K. (1999). Developing practice, developing practitioners: Toward a practice-based theory of professional education. In G. Sykes and L. Darling-Hammond (Eds.), Teaching as the learning profession: Handbook of policy and practice (pp. 3–32). San Francisco: Jossey Bass.

Bell, J. (2015). Essences of growth: Mentoring in education as a community of practice. Unpublished manuscript, Department of Teacher Education, Michigan State University.

Bell, J., Stanulis, R. N., & Macaluso, M. (2016). *A tale of two mentors: Contrasting educative and traditional mentoring in the induction years.* Paper presenting at the annual meeting of AERA, Washington, DC.

Borko, H. (2004). Professional development and teacher learning: Mapping the terrain. *Educational Researcher, 33*(8), 3–15.

Bradbury, L. (2010). Educative mentoring: Promoting reform-based science teaching through mentoring relationships. *Science Education, 94*(6), 1049–1071.

Brondyk, S., & Stanulis, R. N. (2014). Teacher leadership for change. *Kappa Delta Pi Record, 50*(1), 13–17.

Bullough, R. (2009). The continuing education of teachers: Inservice training and workshops. In L. J. Saha & A.G. Dworkin (Eds.), *International handbook of research on teachers and teaching* (pp. 159–169). Springer Science & Business Media LLC. New York, NY.

Cooper, K. S., Stanulis, R. N., Brondyk, S. K., Hamilton, E. R., Macaluso, M., & Meier, J. A. (2016). The teacher leadership process: Attempting change within embedded systems. Journal of Educational Change, *17*(1), 85–113.

Desimone, L. (2009). Improving impact studies of teachers' professional development: Toward better conceptualizations and measures. *Educational Researcher, 38*(3), 181–199.

Drago-Severson, E. (2007). Helping teachers learn: Principals as professional development leaders. *Teachers College Record, 109*(1), 70–125.

DuFour, R. (2004). What is a "professional learning community"? *Schools as Learning Communities, 61*(8), 6–11.

Fairman, J. C., & Mackenzie, S. V. (2015). How teacher leaders influence others and understand their leadership. *International Journal of Leadership in Education*, *18*(1), 61–87.

Feiman-Nemser, S. (1998). Teachers as teacher educators. *European Journal of Teacher Education*, *21*(1), 63–74. Retrieved from http://doi.org/10.1080/0261976980210107

Feiman-Nemser, S. (2001). Helping novices learn to teach lessons from an exemplary support teacher. *Journal of Teacher Education*, *52*(1), 17–30.

Feiman-Nemser, S., & Beasley, K. (1997). Mentoring as assisted performance: A case of co-planning. In V. Richardson (Ed), *Constructivist teacher education* (pp. 108–126). Bristol, PA: The Falmer Press, Taylor & Francis Inc.

Feiman-Nemser, S., & Buchmann, M. (1987). When is student teaching teacher education? *Teacher & Teacher Education*, *3*(4), 255–273.

Gareis, C. R., & Grant, L. W. (2014). The efficacy of training cooperating teachers. *Teaching and Teacher Education*, *39*, 77–88. http://doi.org/10.1016/j.tate.2013.12.007

Hiebert, J., Morris, A. K., Berk, D., & Jansen, A. (2007). Preparing teachers to learn from teaching. *Journal of Teacher Education*, *58*(1), 47–61.

Hobson, A. J., Ashby, P., Malderez, A., & Tomlinson, P. D. (2009). Mentoring beginning teachers: What we know and what we don't. *Teaching and Teacher Education*, *25*(1), 207–216.

Leatham, K. R., & Peterson, B. E. (2010). Secondary mathematics cooperating teachers' perceptions of the purpose of student teaching. *Journal of Mathematics Teacher Education*, *13*(2), 99–119.

Lieberman, A. (2015). Creating the conditions for learning: Teachers as leaders. *The Educational Forum*, *79*(1), 3–4.

Little, J. W. (1990). The mentor phenomenon and the social organization of teaching. *Review of Research in Education*, *16*, 297–351.

Lortie, D. C. (1975). *School teacher: A sociological inquiry*. Chicago, IL: University of Chicago Press.

Norman, P. J., & Feiman-Nemser, S. (2005). Mind activity in teaching and mentoring. *Teacher and Teacher Education*, *21*(6), 679–697.

Pitton, D. E. (2006). *Mentoring novice teachers: Fostering a dialogue process*. Thousand Oaks, CA: Corwin Press.

Pylman, S. (2016). *A "safe place" to inquire and develop as teacher educators: Mentor teacher professional learning communities (PLCs)*. Paper presenting at the annual meeting of AACTE, Las Vegas, NV.

Pylman, S. (2016). Reflecting on Talk: A Mentor Teacher's Gradual Release in Co-Planning. The New Educator, *12*(1), 48–66.

Schon, D. A. (1983). *The reflective practitioner: How professionals think in action*. New York, NY: Basic Books.

Schwille, S. A. (2008). The professional practice of mentoring. *American Journal of Education*, *115*(1), 139–167.

Standards-based protocol for analyzing student work. (n.d.). Retrieved from http://assist.educ.msu.edu/ASSIST/school/together/seciiplc/seciidlrntog/3toolanalysisprots.htm

Stanulis, R. N., & Ames, K. T. (2009). Learning to mentor: Evidence and observation as tools in learning to teach. *Professional Educator*, *33*(1), n1.

Stanulis, R. N., & Bell, J. (2017). Beginning teachers improve with attentive and targeted mentoring. Kappa Delta Pi Record, *53*(2), 59–65.

Stanulis, R. N., & Brondyk, S. K. (2013). Complexities involved in mentoring towards a high leverage practice in the induction years. *Teachers College Record*, *115*(10), 1–34.

Stanulis, R. N., & Brondyk, S. K. (2014, March). Educative debriefing. Presentation for Woodrow Wilson Mentors, John Carroll University, Cleveland, OH.

Stanulis, R. N., Brondyk, S. K., Little, S., & Wibbens, E. (2014). Mentoring beginning teachers to enact discussion-based teaching. *Mentoring & Tutoring: Partnership in Learning*, *22*(2), 127–145. http://doi.org/10.1080/13611267.2014.902556

Stanulis, R. N., Cooper, K. S., Dear, B., Johnston, A. M., & Richard-Todd, R. R. (2016). Teacher-led reforms have a big advantage—teachers. Phi Delta Kappan, *97*(7), 53–57.

Stanulis, R. N., Little, S., & Wibbens, E. (2012). Intensive mentoring that contributes to change in beginning elementary teachers' learning to lead classroom discussions. *Teaching and Teacher Education*, *28*, 32–43.

Stanulis, R. N., Pylman, S.m & Wexler, L. (2015). Mentors as Teacher Educators. *Opening Day Presentation*. Michigan State University, East Lansing, MI.

Timperley, H. (2001). Mentoring conversations designed to promote student teacher learning. *Asia-Pacific Journal of Teacher Education*, *29*(2), 111–123.

Wang, J., & Paine, L. (2001). Mentoring as assisted performance: A pair of Chinese teachers working together. *Elementary School Journal*, *102*(2), 157–181.

Warren-Little, J. (2006). Professional community and professional development in the learning-centered school. *Best Practices NEA Research: Working Paper*. Washington, DC: National Education Association.

Warren-Little, J., Gearhart, M., Curry, M., & Kafka, J. (2003). Looking at student work for teacher learning, teacher community, and school reform. *Phi Delta Kappan*, *83*(3), 184–192.

York-Barr, J., & Duke, K. (2004). What do we know about teacher leadership? Findings from two decades of scholarship. *Review of Educational Research*, *74*(3), 255–316.

Yusko, B., & Feiman-Nemser, S. (2008). Embracing contraries: Combining assistance and assessment in new teacher induction. *The Teachers College Record*, *110*(5), 923–953.

Chapter 2

Transforming Induction

Contexts and Practice

Sandra L. Hardy

ABSTRACT

This chapter explores the process of transforming teacher induction as tailored to the individual teacher's further learning to teach and the perceived environment of the school and district from a new or novice teacher's perspective. This chapter highlights a qualitative study of 18 teachers new to a school district in the Midwest, 11 of them were novice teachers. Each teacher was interviewed individually concerning their perceptions of the current mentoring program to determine what would be most helpful to each teacher in order to assist the central office administration in developing a more formalized induction program with mentoring an integral part of the induction experience. Major themes that emerged from the data included: (a) the need for regular meetings with their mentor, (b) more information on curriculum prior to the start of the school year, (c) more explanation of policies and procedures, (d) classroom management, and (e) the opportunity to collaborate with same grade level teachers. Implications for transforming induction, contexts, and practice are considered.

KEYWORDS

administration, contexts, culture of mentoring, learning community, mentors and mentoring, novice teachers, professional development, teacher induction, teacher leadership, transforming induction programs, university faculty

INTRODUCTION

Teacher induction opportunities greatly enhance and transform the quality of instruction in the attainment of effective education and thereby may increase learner achievement immensely (Korpershock, Harms, Boer, van Kuijk, & Doolaard, 2016). The benefits of well-established and resourced induction programs extend to new and more experienced educators to reach all learners.

This progression in accordance with continuous professional development and support of continued learning through practice accentuates the essential framework of effective induction programs. Further, when well developed and implemented, comprehensive induction experiences link school and university to jointly acknowledge unique qualities at various levels and components of professional development in the contexts of practice.

In this chapter the formal and roles of classroom teachers as associated educators are explored. Such roles are examined within the realm of environmental as well as other contextual elements unique to teachers as learners. Specific consideration is given to the professional learning to teach requirements of new to a school and novice teachers as unique to each circumstance and individual in the development and implementation of transforming induction experiences.

First, the factors of educational culture are considered as environment in district and school contexts. Next, the elemental influence of leaders and leadership in transforming induction programs is infused followed by mentors and mentoring. Then, novices' and new teachers' professional development objectives pertaining to transforming induction programs are illuminated. The afore mentioned core concepts are further captured and illustrated through a snapshot qualitative study of the induction needs of 18 new teachers to a school district as part of the transformation of that induction program for those teachers at that time. Finally, the essential focal points to transforming induction programs are encapsulated and dispersed through implications and summary.

Well-developed and implemented induction experiences have the potential to shape education in theory and in practice for future generations (Moir & Gless, 2001). Induction in connection to other professional development activities perpetuates the evolving transformations of further learning to teach through practice and reflection of classroom teachers as associated teacher educators.

The repercussions bring to task the fundamental education repositories to reinforce professional networks across the further learning to teach spectrum. Classroom teachers as teacher educators are found near and far. The parameters include but are not limited to the close immediate proximity of the classroom teacher across the hall to the far-reaching, globally encompassing technological extensions of educators on computers beyond the boundaries of time and space.

Classroom teachers as associated teacher educators serve pervasively throughout formal and informal structures of social relations in peer support that both allure and promote teachers. However, obviously not all induction programs and learning to teach environments are the same in the support they offer new and novice educators to retain them (Mills, Moore, & Keane, 2001).

Established and well-maintained networks attract prepared educators and encourage teachers to remain in the profession. Such programs provide professional and interpersonal support that fosters teacher retention and professional development (Blair-Larsen, 1998; Scherer, 2001). Finding and retaining well-prepared teachers is critical to the profession as many teachers continue to retire or enter another career (Freiberg, 2000).

Classroom teachers as associated teacher educators give voice as professionals who strengthen learning through induction practices. Further, the network formed encompasses classroom teachers in various aspects of their development, including the role of teacher educators in support of their peers at all stages of their career. There are multiple pathways through which teachers can connect to professional principles that anchor and retain valued educators in the midst of shifting content and processes to attain academic balance in terms of achievement on a local, national, and increasingly international scale.

To establish an effective induction program defines the practice of educational objectives to be attained based on the learning and teaching needs of teachers and students (Sweeny & DeBolt, 2000). The nine standards from the Association of Teacher Educators (ATE) highlight guiding principles which anchor and expand professional development in communication and practice (Association of Teacher Educators, n.d.).

Therefore, in implementing these standards, teacher induction respectfully recognizes classroom teachers as associated teacher educators in shared commitment of purpose and vision. The shape this process takes in practice varies from school to school, classroom to classroom, and teacher to teacher. Nonetheless, the key elements of cultural context, leaders and leadership, mentors and mentoring, and professional development remain central in defining the basic framework of transforming all effective induction efforts.

TRANSFORMING INDUCTION: CULTURE AND CONTEXT

Transforming induction involves increased awareness and attention to professional culture and contexts of educational environments regarding the valued resources of teachers as learners in schools and universities internal and external to the organization of the learning institution. The professional aspect of this effort unfolds in multiple perspectives respective to the complexity of meeting the challenges inherent therein (Hargreaves & Fullan, 2000). The context in which learning and teaching are experienced contributes to and greatly influences constructing and reconstructing constructs to reframe meaning in professional discourse and practice.

All schools have a culture that is unique in many ways, fluid in some, unchanging in others. The cultures of educational organizations in practice are the result of progress and traditions. The contexts of the culture in learning resonate internally and externally to permeate the connection intricately tied to value systems. What is valued as worthy of time and given priority attention is where resources are invested. Highly effective professional educators are such a resource.

All education professionals at any point in their career will experience the culture of the school. Novices in particular will take note of the cultural contexts or learning environment through formal and informal induction experiences as they are encultured and encounter working with individuals with various learning needs (Halford, 1998). For some, cultural context of learning environments is noticeable when you pull into the parking lot, others find evidence in the hall while classes are in session and again at break, or on the playground just before the bell rings.

The culture of learning internally and externally to the organization represents the fundamental values that transcend everyday activities. Highly effective induction centrally valued defines the culture of the learning inside, outside, and across educational institutions and requires sufficient attention and commitment to time and other limited resources.

Learning to teach in practice is influenced by the social and environmental nuances that define the larger overall system of highly effective education (Newcombe, 1988). Mentors and other support staff assist the novice or new member to the social network so that they are not overwhelmed, inundated, and swallowed whole by the existing cultural context (Sullivan & Glanz, 2000). Therefore, careful consideration of the current school culture is evident in the development, implementation, and subsequent transformation of induction programs. Such efforts merge purposefully with other similar initiatives and combine to reinforce the culminating processes of improved instruction and the ultimate goal of increased learner achievement (Newcombe, 1988; Robbins, 1999).

Classroom teachers as associated teacher educators are learners, and administrators are teachers. Organizations that strive to be learning institutions defined in practice recognize that induction can and should enhance the development of everyone in that organization (Kelly, Beck, & Thomas,

1992; Yost, 2000). The school's entire faculty and staff are ideally well informed about all aspects of induction as part of professional development efforts (Ganser, 2001). Consequently, there is a cohesive working together, a teacher-to-teacher learning mentality.

When carefully planned and implemented, induction programs for beginning teachers provide a safe environment for further learning to teach (Ganser, 1998). University faculty and staff may serve as a vast, as of yet largely untapped, resource to be engaged from the very beginning of the planning and development through implementation and evaluation phases in transforming induction. Novice practitioners in all arenas and levels benefit from university faculty guidance to practice what they have learned in preparation and stay abreast of current research and practice developments.

School and university teamwork brings increased awareness of school culture and context in connection to vision and mission of professional development and learner achievement. Building and sustaining these partnerships in culture and context serves to define, redefine, and align common goals to purposefully unite efforts and extend resources with commitment to transform the induction experience and process.

TRANSFORMING INDUCTION: LEADERS AND LEADERSHIP

Teachers and administrators as formal and informal leaders provide leadership to transform induction through location and allocation of resources and other forms of support. Leaders inspire teachers and others to implement transformational changes brought about through high expectations of self in learning and teaching environments that is conducive to accepting the responsibility of attaining these objectives (Hitt & Tucker, 2016). Induction is a priority for highly effective leaders (Sweeny, 2001). All aspects of the induction process are connected to the level of support found in formal and informal leadership.

Leadership in areas of instruction is frequently emphasized in school reform agendas (Hatch, Hill, & Roegman, 2016). Leadership can be illustrated in the practice of teachers and staff and is not relegated to formal roles of administration (Hitt & Tucker, 2016). Classroom teachers as associated teacher educators are informal leaders and, when given a title, are formal teacher leaders who may take a more formal path of instructional leadership through preparation.

Teachers and other formal and informal leaders are best prepared with a substantial knowledge base, a firm belief system, and commitment to induction as benefiting practice. These beliefs are communicated intentional or not, and permeate the dynamic processes throughout. Therefore it is absolutely essential in transforming an induction program to first induct well-integrated instructional and transformational leaders (Hitt & Tucker, 2016).

Administration

Administrators as formal leaders will direct professional development toward their own improvements along with other staff after motivating teachers with the purpose of effective education (Hitt & Tucker, 2016). Induction efforts benefit from creative, full-time program administrators with the time and resources to direct adequate attention supporting novices (Moir & Gless, 2001) on a daily basis (Ganser, 2001). One significant factor in the process of learning more about teaching and learning in the school is the establishment of routines that encourage effective communication among teachers and administrators across classrooms and buildings (Hatch et al., 2016).

Financial resources vary, and accordingly, alterations occur creatively to custom fit and tailor the specific needs uniquely suited to individuals in each learning community. Some learning communities have professional development directors who will be directly responsible for the induction program in many respects. This is an ideal situation, but not all schools can afford to hire a professional development director. Other communities have one administrator who is the superintendent and the principal, the curriculum coordinator, and the professional development director.

Perhaps most importantly, the administration is effectively aware and acts on behalf of the current learning to teach culture of their school in promoting the transformation of induction. Highly effective administrators are aware how and why induction thrives in their building, and they strive to make systemic improvements as a healthy extension of the pervasive professional development of classroom teachers as associated teacher educators.

The administration extends many levels of support for the success of transforming induction programs. Administrative backing includes pairing the best match for mentor and novice (Ganser, 1996; Hillkirk & Murray, 1998). Location for accessibility is an important factor to consider. The veteran teacher and novice should ideally be in close proximity and working with the same type of students (Lloyd, Wood, Moreno, & Gerardo, 2000). The building principal is a very influential leader in determining the importance of induction in their building and the role of mentor (Olsen, 1989). The building principal often decides novice and mentor pairings and location.

Although it is important that all administrators take responsibility for the development of a novice, the role of the building principal is probably the most critical (Portner, 2001). The building administrator communicates to staff the importance of induction and that everyone has a role to play. Further, the building administrator assists in providing time for the mentor and novice to meet, releasing the mentor to observe the novice and the novice to observe the mentor or another veteran teacher (Wollman-Bonilla, 1997) to improve instruction (Wood & Killian, 1998).

Observations provide feedback that benefits novice and mentor to shape and improve their practice (Cohen & Goldhaber, 2016). Principals and other administrators and staff can cover classes and provide many forms of adequate support to make the experience of observing one another possible and meaningful for teachers.

Formal and informal leaders as teachers and administrators serve in multiple capacities to transform induction programs. Leaders provide leadership in assigning time, space, and other essential resources to meet the professional development needs of classroom teachers as associated teacher educators. The induction transformation with strong, creative leadership and adequate resources enhances all faculty and staff while improving the learning to teach culture and context in the process.

TRANSFORMING INDUCTION: MENTORS AND MENTORING

Effective teachers realize that they will continue professional development throughout their practice (Bartell, Kaye, & Morin, 1998). Induction should be an integral part of a larger plan, so that mentors and first-year teachers are involved in a seamless continuum of professional growth (McKenna, 1998). Mentors and mentoring transform induction through mentor preparation that blends continuously into other professional development efforts that address individual novice and mentor career and learning to teach needs.

Mentoring relationships are found historically in the arts, business, religion, and education, including but not limited to apprenticeships (Haak & Smith, 2000). Mentoring relationships require time to be real and reflective in the context of authenticity. The benefits of mentoring extend beyond novices to experienced teachers and reform efforts (Williams & Bowman, 2000).

Induction recognizes the essential element of formal mentor training as a prerequisite to mentoring (Holloway, 2001; Rowley, 1999). The importance of training mentor teachers arises from the presumption that even excellent veteran classroom teachers have limited experience in working with adults and may not have all the skills and knowledge necessary to become mentors (Odell, 1999). A well-prepared mentor brings a positive perspective to the novice (Rowley, 1999).

The qualities attributed to formal mentors can be just as evident in informal mentors (Tillman, 2000). The learning of what it takes to be a mentor and what novices need to know is part of professional development and is, to an extent, individualized even though some constructs are common throughout. Mentor training is needed to promote effective mentorship. Mentor training is continuous.

It is not a one-day in-service or even a five-day in-service. Mentor training should never be a one-shot in-service. It should be an ongoing process of instruction, interaction, sharing, support, and reflection that begins before school starts and continues throughout the year (McKenna, 1998). Upon completion of such training the mentor and novice may work as a team to forge an individualized plan of professional development for the novice teacher (Mills et al., 2001; Steadman & Stroot, 1998).

Mentoring can greatly influence a novice's career path (Stanulis & Weaver, 1998). Research on mentoring in private industry and corporations reveals a high correlation between professional success and positive mentoring experiences (Madison & Hutson, 1996). As all teachers are potentially mentors at some point in their careers, the entire faculty would benefit from an overview of mentoring and what is required of an effective mentorship.

Trust. An element of trust is found in successful mentoring experiences (Peterson & Williams, 1998).Trust is essential to the school climate through teachers' communications to enhance support and lessen stress factors as a result of changes. Furthermore, trust creates an atmosphere more conducive to reflection and reflective practice (Weasmer & Woods, 1999).

The profoundly positive impact of peer mentoring on professional development ripples through the culture of the educational community to improve learner achievement. Therefore, it may be advantageous to initiate peer mentoring as a natural outgrowth of the culture building to open channels of communication, increase understandings, and deepen a level of trust inside and outside of the organization.

Unfortunately, in some instances there are occasionally teachers who are reluctant to accept the newly recognized formal mentors as peers (Shulman & Colbert, 1987). This causes a cultural affect that raises tension and animosity. Proactively, peer mentoring is a way to practice mentoring, to learn a great deal from one's colleagues, and to reduce the likelihood of this lack of acceptance or of resisting the status of a mentor in the group.

Autonomy. Autonomy is to be respected. Each teacher at all stages of their career is an individual with unique qualities of strengths and areas they desire to improve upon as they continue to develop professionally. Classroom teachers as associated teacher educators will have ideas that are created as they experience growth and learning from their peers. Peer coaching or mentoring from classroom teachers as associated teacher educators is often effective as time with individual teachers is crucial to promoting their professional development (Moore, 2000).

Reflection and focus. Taking time to reflect clarifies concerns of what constitutes professional practice. Reflection paves the way to initiate and propagate mentoring. A mentor may start with reflecting upon his or her experiences as a novice, the formal and informal mentors he or she had, what those experiences were like, what would have made him or her better. Reflection is the heart of mentoring. Mentors serve as role models in reflecting upon their prior learning to teach experiences (Cheney, 1999).

To be a mentor is not only embracing the concept of mentoring and create a caring context, but also employs the pedagogy needed to carry out that commitment (Silva & Tom, 2001). Mentors are preferably available in time and proximity for regular meetings with the novice. Mentors need to be made aware of the need for frequent contact and to "check in" with the beginning teachers and provide support on at least a weekly basis (Whitaker, 2000).

The role of the mentor is that of supporter and facilitator. The initial days and weeks are critical to the mentor–novice relationship (Steadman & Stroot, 1998). Mentors need to take the first step to create a collaborative, colleague-to-colleague learning relationship (Denmark & Podsen, 2000). Mentors are expected to make the first phone call, start the first conversation, and extend himself or herself to the novice. Mentors determine to a great extent the tone of the mentoring relationship in these beginning encounters (Zachary, 2000). As a mentor develops mentoring skills, there are multitudes of side-tracking issues that may arise and cause the focus of the mentoring to be unclear. Focus needs to be revisited with clarity of purpose in supporting the novice to transform their practice as to improve student learning (Portner, 1998).

Not all teachers think alike. Some newer teachers as well as some more experienced teachers may have very different ways of viewing particular constructs. Therefore, it is advantageous to maintain an open posture, to listen with an open mind and, an open heart. Mentoring is apt to evoke enhanced professional autonomy (Sullivan & Glanz, 2000).

A mentor offers insight, guidance, feedback, problem-solving, and a network of colleagues who share resources, insights, practices, and materials. This circle of support is a lifeline to an individual new to teaching, or new to a building, who may otherwise find themselves overwhelmed in the transformation (Robbins, 1999).

A mentor is ideally not judgmental of beliefs and the potential skills of the novice in creating contextually rich environments in which the practice can be refined (Peterson & Williams, 1998) or redefined. For risk taking to occur and growth to result, there is a sense of safety, or trust and openness. Consequently, it is advised that under no circumstances is a mentor to be in a position of evaluative stance. Mentors honor confidentiality and instill trust as professionals. They do not relay information to the principal as to influence evaluation. Mentors are not evaluators.

Mentors accept the novice from where they are and move them at a pace and manner, point in time, that promotes professional growth. They do not clone themselves. It's not a cookie cutter mentality. Autonomy, individuality, the art of teaching, all respected. Perhaps refined, but still respected. Obviously placing mentors in the position to evaluate the novice could present many challenges for the mentoring experience (Troutman, 2000). Administrators need to be aware to not jeopardize the mentoring relationship and respect the confidentiality of the mentorship completely. The mentor's role is facilitator, not evaluator (Lloyd et al., 2000).

Conflict is inevitable as the relationship grows and the mentor and novice learn and grow individually both personally and professionally. The potential exists for strife between differing expectations and needs as the relationship progresses which may lead to conflict (Campbell & Campbell, 2000). Mentoring carries the potential to rise above miscommunications with transforming those times of misunderstanding into opportunities for growth (Hiemstra & Brockett, 1998). The process of mentoring benefits the mentor, novice, and peers (Wollman-Bonilla, 1997).

An effective mentor gladly serves as a resource to expand perspectives and open opportunities by introducing the novice to connections in the teaching profession and in the context internal and external to the learning organization. Mentors are in that respect a guide who fosters tremendous potential for growth and themselves develop professionally as a result of their commitment to the process. It is up to the novice to accept the gift of learning in this manner. Then, they, too, may become mentors and the cycle renews itself building the professional culture of education each time classroom teachers are recognized as associated teacher educators. Mentors and mentoring transform induction through preparation and practice in respecting autonomy and trust in the reflection of focus.

TRANSFORMING INDUCTION: NOVICES AND PROFESSIONAL DEVELOPMENT

The first 4 years of teaching comprise the duration of a teacher's professional development as a novice. The novice stage is critical as a time period in which a teacher learns many strategies and habits that influence both their decision to remain in the profession and the degree of effectiveness displayed in teacher they will become. Teachers who routinely are reflective are continuously searching for ways to improve their practice (Olebe, Jackson, & Danielson, 1999). For the novice, professional development integrates acquiring skills and new strategies and integrating these tools into reflective practice (Boreen, Johnson, Niday, & Potts, 2000).

There are many methods of obtaining new strategies such as through coursework, workshops, mentoring, peers, and observing other teachers.

Observing other teachers is a powerful learning experience (William & Bowman, 2000). Novices often struggle with transferring and establishing effective classroom management skills into their practice. Observation of other teachers offers the opportunity to expand a novice's repertoire of classroom management techniques (Brainard, 2001).

So as to allow for the professional autonomy and development of each teacher it is essential to consider the needs of the novice common to all novices as well as the uniqueness of the individual. An educator enters the realm of teaching with varied levels and sorts of experiences both personally and professionally.

Some may be beginning a second career, while others are just out of college and beginning their first official place of employment in the school district. Particular areas of concern are discipline and management skills, curriculum and lesson planning, school routines and scheduling, motivational techniques, and individualized instruction (David, 2000). Sensitivity to teacher individuality in the context of what all novices require reveals skills and knowledge to be addressed in highly effective professional development.

TRANSFORMING INDUCTION: "A SNAPSHOT IN TIME" QUALITATIVE STUDY

The needs of the novice, new teachers, and mentor teachers are important to take into account in transforming induction. Opinions and needs from the teachers are important to validate in program development, implementation, and evaluation. Once the induction program has been implemented, evaluation determines its effectiveness and indicates areas that need to be improved. This is a continuous process. As an illustration of one caveat in this process, a snapshot of one district's mentoring program improvement goals is presented in an overview of the following qualitative study.

METHODOLOGY

In the effort to improve induction programs, it is important to consider both informal and formal methods of evaluation procedures when gathering relevant information. One qualitative methodology of data collection applied in this study is the face-to-face interview. While time consuming, the insured confidentiality of the interviews brought about more important information from many perspectives (Isaac & Michael, 1997).

PARTICIPANTS

As part of program development to formalize a mentoring program in a Midwest K-12 school district, all 18 newly hired teachers were interviewed concerning what areas of mentoring program could be improved to better meet their learning to teach needs. The study was approved by human subjects prior to beginning the research. All participants gave written consent to participate with the understanding that the data would be used for research purposes.

The participants' prior teaching experience ranged from 0 to 24 years. Of those 18 teachers interviewed, 11 were novices. The teachers were interviewed individually in their respective classrooms. They selected dates and times that were best for them from a selection of time slots provided by the researcher. All of these teachers had been assigned an informal mentor. All of the teachers agreed to participate with the understanding their identity would remain confidential. Respondents were assured of anonymity, and it was explained that only with their prior consent would some of the data would be shared with the central office staff for program improvement purposes only.

RESEARCHER

The researcher conducted the research as part of her doctoral program internship in which she worked very closely with the assistant superintendent of curriculum and instruction in the district in which she taught. The researcher had the support of the district administration in designing and implementing the study in order to gather information from new and novice teachers concerning their needs from a formal mentoring program. Further, the data were to be obtained with the understanding that confidentiality would be strictly upheld for all participants.

INTERVIEW AND RESEARCH QUESTIONS

When meeting with each teacher, the purpose of the interview was explained to obtain information to improve the school district's mentoring program for future teachers and that their help was very important. The participating teachers were assured that this was not connected to their evaluation, and that the focus was on improving the mentoring program by meeting the needs of new teachers in the district.

The four research and program development questions were typed on a form and read aloud to each teacher. The researcher recorded the teachers'

Table 2.1. Participant Information

					Themes		
# Years Teaching	Subject/Grade Taught	Prior Mentor	Regular Meetings with Mentor	More Info. on the Curriculum Prior to Starting	Procedures and Policies	Classroom Management	Meet with Grade Level Teachers
5	P.E. Elem.	no	yes	Yes			
3	Kindergarten	yes	yes		yes		yes
0	4th grade	no	yes				yes
1	2nd grade	no	yes	Yes			
1	1st grade	yes	yes	Yes			
4	Primary B.D.	yes		Yes	yes		
4	Pre-K	no	yes				
1	S.S. 7th and 8th	yes	yes		yes		
0	2nd grade	no		Yes	yes	yes	
0	5th gr. R.E.I.	no	yes		yes	yes	yes
0	Art (k-6)	no			yes		
1	P.E. 7th and 8th	no	yes		yes		
5	7–12th Chorus	no	yes		yes		
24	H.S./L.D.	no	yes		yes	yes	
16	H.S./P.E.	no	yes		yes	yes	
13	Kindergarten	yes			yes		
13	4th grade	no	yes		yes		yes
22	REI 4th grade	yes	yes				

responses verbatim. The interview consisted of four questions, with follow-up probing questions for clarity.

RQ 1: How long have you been teaching?

RQ 2: What were your previous teaching assignments?

RQ 3: Have you had a formal mentor before and if so please elaborate on that experience?

RQ 4: As a new teacher to this district what would be most helpful to you from a formal mentor?

Table 2.1 presents the level of teaching experience, subject or grade taught, whether or not they had a mentor prior to the year they were hired into the district, and the five emergent categories of themes. The central theme reflected what the teachers perceived as most helpful from a formal mentor based on their responses to the four research questions.

DATA ANALYSIS

The participants' comments to each research question were recorded verbatim. This included probing and follow-up questions and responses for clarity. The resulting data were then analyzed and cross analyzed for emergent themes and subthemes based on the participants' responses.

FINDINGS

The results of the interviews consisting of the research questions and follow-up probing questions indicated several significant themes. Focusing on the novice and new to the district teachers' perceptions and their individual further learning to teach needs from their mentor. The discoveries emerged as a needs assessment for this school district in developing in-service for a more formalized mentoring program. Results indicate the following for these teachers in this specific school district and may also be applicable to other new and novice teachers in other contexts:

1. Only 6 of the 18 participants had former experience with a mentor.
2. The majority of those interviewed, 14 of 18 indicated they would like regular meetings with their mentor. Those teachers who were in close proximity met more often or even shared office space was a factor in how often they met a few minutes or more with their mentor.

3. More information on the curriculum prior to starting the school year was indicated by 5 of the 18 teachers.
4. There was a significant need for more information on procedures and policies with 12 of the 18 teachers new to this district.
5. Only 4 of the 18 expressed a need for assistance from mentoring with classroom management.
6. Only 4 of the 18 teachers showed a need for meeting with other grade-level teachers.

Statements from the participants are provided to assist the reader in uncovering predominant themes (Rubin & Rubin, 1995). The following are some pertinent comments from the novice teachers and new teachers to this school district:

- "Paper work ahead of time to keep a record of questions—concerns before meeting with my mentor, instead of trying to keep them in your head—this would only be between teacher and mentor—maybe the mentor would have one too."
- "It's the little things, how to use the copy machine, what paper to use."
- "Meet one on one before the first day so you know what to expect."
- "Conferencing with parents, how to say things to parents."
- "Sharing space helps to talk to the mentor more often."
- "More time with the mentor, time set aside just for that purpose."
- "Observing other teachers now to learn from them would be more helpful to me now than when I was in my teacher education program."
- "It must be real, nothing artificial."

The predominant themes that emerged from the interviews reflected areas in need of improvement to transform induction in this school district for these teachers. It is important to emphasize that these data and the subsequent findings represent a snapshot in time from the perspective of these 18 teachers. The answers to these same questions may have yielded different results with another group of teachers, in another district, or at another time in the school year.

Each induction program to be highly effective takes into account the individual needs of the teachers in the context and culture of the school and district. Given the goal to build a strong teaching profession, every school has the responsibility to the teachers it hires to provide well-prepared mentors. The teaching profession depends upon well-prepared and supported teachers who are ready to face the challenges ahead while also continuing professional development efforts with the guidance of mentor teachers as associated teacher educators (Morgan, 1999).

IMPLICATIONS

The study effort represents only a snapshot in time of the overall picture of this particular district's induction program for these teachers at that time. Therefore, the implications are pertinent in the transformation of the induction program for this particular district in terms of giving voice to the needs of the specific new and novice teachers who participated in this study. The school district had the goal of learning the needs of the new and novice teachers in order to formalize their existing mentoring program.

Therefore, the insights gleaned from these interviews were significant in that regard. Furthermore, the use of interview and other research and evaluation tools to better understand the needs of classroom teachers as associated teacher educators is applicable to all further learning to teach endeavors. Certainly consideration is given to the context and culture of the educational organization internally and externally.

LIMITATIONS

While the perceptions of the novice and new teachers are valuable, so too are the voices of the mentor teachers, other teachers, building administrators, and central office administration. Additionally, the keen insight and expertise of higher education teacher educators would have also brought a knowledgeable vantage point. Consequently, the findings of this study would have been further enhanced had mentors, administrators, and higher education teacher educators also been interviewed. Such information would serve to reveal in what respects the perceptions were similar or distinct concerning the further learning to teach needs of novice and new teachers and the role of mentors and administrators.

SUMMARY

Induction programs carry the capacity to support the development of novices as well as all members of the learning to teach educational enterprise to increase learner achievement. Cultural contexts of learning environments present opportunities and challenges to tailor induction experiences that adequately meet the needs of the individual teachers and schools in terms of resources.

Mentor teachers and administrators benefit from preparation from higher education educators linking preparation to practice as to their role in the induction process. Beginning teachers greatly benefit from the support and facilitation of well-prepared mentors and administrators. Thus, it is necessary to determine exactly what areas of improvement are most desired as essential to transform induction.

Induction programs often focus on teaching teachers how to provide feedback to novices (Halford, 1998). Classroom teachers as associated teacher educators value constructive feedback as part of professional development (Stanulis & Weaver, 1998).

However, each program is unique in the careful consideration to the individual and cumulative professional development needs of teachers and the special learning considerations of students in the contexts of time and other valuable resources. The allocation of resources influences how the induction program reinforces other professional development and school improvement efforts. Therefore, variability in planning and implementation occurs to allow for authenticity of mentors (Bell, 1997) and of the individual teacher as associated teacher educator and learner to transform induction, contexts, and practice.

REFERENCES

Association of Teacher Educators. (n.d.). *Standards for teacher educators*. Retrieved from http://www.ate1.org/pubs/uploads/tchredstdst0308.pdf

Bartel, C., Kaye, C., & Morin, J. (1998, winter). Portfolio conversation: A mentored journey. *Teacher Education Quarterly, 25*(1), 129–139.

Bell, C. (1997, February). The bluebird's secret: Mentoring with bravery and balance. *Training and Development, 51*, 30–33.

Blair-Larsen, S. M. (1998, Summer). Designing a mentoring program. *Education, 118* (4), 602–604.

Boreen, J., Johnson, M. K., Niday, D., & Potts, J. (2000). Mentoring beginning teachers, guiding, reflecting, coaching. *How do I encourage professional development?* (pp. 85–99). York, MA: Stenhouse Publishers.

Brainard, E. (2001, April). Classroom management: Seventy-three suggestions for secondary school teachers. *The Clearing House, 74*(4), 207–210.

Campbell, D. E., & Campbell, T. A. (2000, December). The mentoring relationship: Differing perceptions of benefits. *College Student Journal, 34* (4), 516–523.

Cheney, D. (1999, August). Mentorship in the field of behavioral disorders: An intergenerational responsibility. *Education and the Treatment of Children, 22* (3), 234–243.

Cohen, J., & Goldhaber, D. (2016). Building a more complete understanding of teacher evaluation using classroom observations. *Educational Researcher, 45*(6), 378–387.

David, T. (2000, Spring). Teacher mentoring—Benefits all around. *Kappa Delta Pi Record, 36*(3), 134–136.

Denmark, V. M., & Podsen, I. J. (2000, Fall). The mettle of a mentor. *Journal of Staff Development, 21*(4), 18–22.

Freiberg, M. R., (2000, October). Coaching and mentoring first-year and student teachers. *NASSP Bulletin, 84*(618), 87–88.

Ganser, T. (1996, Summer). What do mentors say about mentoring? *Journal of Staff Development, 17*, 36–39.

Ganser, T. (1998, Winter). Metaphors for mentoring. *The Educational Forum, 62*, 113–119.

Ganser, T. (2001, Winter). The principal as new teacher mentor. *Journal of Staff Development, 22* (1), 39–41.

Halford, J. M. (1998, February). Easing the way for new teachers. *Educational Leadership, 55*, 33–36.

Hargreaves, A., & Fullan, M. (2000, Winter). Mentoring in the new millennium. *Theory into Practice, 39*(1), 50–56.

Hatch, T., Hill, K., & Roegman, R. (2016). Investigating the role of instructional rounds in the development of social networks and district-wide improvement. *American Education Research Journal, 53*(4), 1022–1053.

Hiemstra, R., & Brockett, R. G. (1998, Fall). From mentor partner: Lessons from a personal journey. *New Directions for Adult and Continuing Education, 79*, 43–51.

Hillkirk, K., & Murray, S. R. (1998). *Entry Year Pilot Project: A Reflective Approach to Mentoring Ohio's Entry Year Teacher* (Chapter Eight, P. 48). A monograph presented to the Ohio Department of Education, Ohio University, College of Education.

Hitt, D. H., & Tucker, P.D. (2016). Systemic review of key leader practices found to influence student achievement: A unified framework. *Review of Educational Research, 86*(2), 531–569.

Hollway, J. H. (2001, May). The benefits of mentoring. *Educational Leadership, 58*(8), 85–86.

Isaac, S., & Michael, W. B.(1997). *Handbook in research and evaluation* (3rd ed.), San Diego, CA: EdITS.

Kelly, M., Beck, T., & Thomas, J. (1992). Mentoring as a staff development activity. In M. Wilkin (Ed.), *Mentoring in schools* (pp. 173–180). London: Kogan Page Limited.

Korpershock, H., Harms, T., Boer, H., van Kuijk, M., & Doolard, S. (2016). A meta-analysis of the effects of classroom management strategies and classroom management programs on students' academic, behavioral, emotional, and motivational outcomes. *Review of Educational Research, 88*(3), 643–680.

Lloyd, S., Wood, R., Moreno, T, & Gerardo, A. (2000, September/October). What's a mentor to do? *Teaching Exceptional Children, 33*(1), 38–42.

Madison, J., & Huston, C. (1996, Summer). Faculty-faculty mentoring relationships: An American and Australian perspective. *NASPA Journal, 33*, 316–330.

McKenna, G. (1998, January). Mentor training: The key to effective staff development. *Principal, 77*, 47–49.

Mills, H., Moore, D., & Keane, W. (2001, January, February). Addressing the teacher shortage: A study of successful mentoring programs in Oakland county, Michigan. *The Clearing House, 74*(3), 124–126.

Moir, E., & Gless, J. (2001, Winter). Quality induction: An investment in teachers. *Teacher Education Quarterly, 28*(1), 109–114.

Moore, K. B. (2000, November/December). Successful & effective professional development. *Scholastic Early Childhood Today, 15*(3), 14–16.

Morgan, B. M. (1999, Spring). Passing the torch: Performance assessment benchmarks for preservice teachers and mentor teacher training. *Education, 119*(3), 374–380.

Newcombe, E. (1988). *Mentoring programs for new teachers.* Philadelphia, PA: Research for Better Schools.

Olebe, M., Jackson, A., & Danielson, C. (1999, May). Investing in beginning teachers— The California model. *Educational Leadership, 56*(8), 41–44.

Olsen, K. D. (1989). *The mentor teacher role: Owner's manual* (5th ed.). Village of Oak Creek, AZ: Books for Educators.

Peterson, B. E., & Williams, S. R. (1998, November). Mentoring beginning teachers. *Mathematics Teacher, 91*(8), 730–734.

Portner, H., (1998). *Mentoring new teachers* (p. 75). Thousand Oaks, CA: Sage.

Portner, H., (2001). *Training mentors is not enough, everything else schools and districts need to do.* Thousand Oaks, CA: Cowin Press, Inc.

Robbins, P. (1999, Summer). Mentoring. *Journal of Staff Development, 20*(3), 40–42.

Rowley, J. B.(1999). The good mentor. *Association of Supervision and Curriculum Development, 56*(8), 20-22.

Rowley, J. B. (1999, May). The good mentor. *Educational Leadership, 56*(8), 20–22.

Rubin, H. L., & Rubin, I. S. (1995). *Qualitative interviewing: The art of hearing data.* Thousand Oaks, CA: Sage Publications

Scherer, M. (2001, May). Improving the quality of the teaching force: A conversation with David C. Berliner. *Educational Leadership, 58*(8), 6–10.

Shulman, J. H., & Colbert, J. A. (1987). *The mentor teacher casebook* (p. 84), Far West Laboratory for Educational Research and Development and Eric Clearinghouse on Educational Management University of Oregon.

Silva, D. Y. & Tom, A. R. (2001, Spring). The moral basis of mentoring. *Teacher Education Quarterly, 28*(2), 39–52.

Stanulis, R. N., & Weaver, D. (1998, Autumn). Teacher as mentor, teacher as learner: Lessons from a middle-school language arts teacher. *The Teacher Educator, 34*(2), 134–143.

Steadman, P., & Stroot, S. A. (1998, February). Teachers helping teachers. *Educational Leadership, 55,* 37–38.

Sullivan, S., & Glanz, J. (2000, Spring). Alternative approaches to supervision: Cases from the field. *Journal of Curriculum and Supervision, 15*(3) 212–235.

Sweeny, B. (2001). *Taking a closer look: Best practices for continuous, high impact teacher development.* Wheaton, IL: Best Practice Resources.

Sweeny, B., & DeBolt, G. (2000). A survey of the 50 states: Mandated teacher-induction programs. In S. Odell & L. Huling (Eds.), *Quality mentoring for novice teachers* (pp. 97–106). Washington, DC: Association of Teacher Educators and Kappa Delta Pi.

Tillman, B. A. (2000, February, March). Quiet leadership: Informal mentoring of beginning teachers. *Momentum (Washington, D.C.), 31*(1), 24–26.

Troutman, P. L., Jr. (2000). *Mentoring, social interaction, and transformations*. Overview and framework. Division III. In D. John McIntyre & David M. Byrd (Eds.), *Research on effective models for teacher education, teacher education yearbook VIII* (pp. 132–135).Thousand Oaks, CA: Corwin Press, Inc.

Weasmer, J., & Woods, A. M. (1999, Fall). Peer partnering for change. *Kappa Delta Pi Record, 36*(1), 32–34.

Whitaker, S. D. (2000, September, October) What do first-year special education teachers need? *Teaching Exceptional Children, 33*(1), 28–36.

Williams, D. A., & Bowman, C. L. (2000). Reshaping the profession one teacher at a time. Collaborative mentoring of entry year teachers. In John McIntyre & David M. Byrd (Eds.), *Research on effective models for teacher education, teacher education yearbook VII* (pp. 173–187). Thousand Oaks, CA: Corwin Press, Inc.

Wollman-Bonilla, J. E. (1997, Summer). Mentoring as a two way street. *Journal of Staff Development, 18*, 50–52.

Wood, F., & Killian, J. (1998, Winter). Job-embedded learning makes the difference in school improvement. *Journal of Staff Development, 19*, 52–54.

Yost, R. (2000, Fall). Learning from the past. *Educational Horizons, 79*(1), 27–30.

Zachary, L. J. (2000). *The mentor's guide*, San Francisco, CA: Jossey-Bass.

Chapter 3

Teachers Learning Together at Auburn Elementary

Supporting Classroom Teachers as Associated Teacher Educators

Cynthia Carver, Marcia Hudson, Molly Abbott, Sarah Bruha, Colleen Bugaj, Jennifer Johnson, and Serena Stock

ABSTRACT

Interest has surged in clinical-based teacher preparation. In this chapter, we add to the discussion by arguing the importance of supportive clinical practice sites, specifically sites that embrace a learning-oriented culture with field-based teacher leaders (as associated teacher educators) who see themselves as continuous learners and model an inquiry stance for their field placement students. Using the example of Teacher Lab, a job-embedded form of professional learning, carefully crafted professional learning practices can provide teachers with rich opportunities for learning skills that ultimately support and enhance their work with preservice teachers.

KEYWORDS

Field-based teacher education, job-embedded professional learning, teacher inquiry

> Children grow into the intellectual life around them.—Lev Vygotsky, Mind & Society

Field-based teacher preparation does not happen in a vacuum but is inherently situated in an existing organizational culture. Is that school culture, however, one that embraces, rejects, or is indifferent to the learning needs of its teachers? At Auburn Elementary, a partnership school with Oakland University (OU), our goal is to ensure that teacher candidates experience a vibrant professional culture and climate where ongoing and collaborative professional learning is modeled daily by classroom teacher leaders. In this rich learning environment preservice teachers thrive.

Supporting this learning environment is Teacher Lab, a job-embedded form of professional learning that is well established at Auburn Elementary. Loosely modeled after lesson study, with added elements from book club and professional learning communities (PLCs), Teacher Lab is widely viewed as the foundation upon which Auburn's collaborative professional culture was built. Today, this foundation nurtures a steady flow of preservice teachers in and out of the building.

In this chapter, Auburn teachers share their experience of Teacher Lab, including the ways in which Teacher Lab has supported their work with preservice teachers while also nurturing a learning-oriented building culture. The value of studying existing programs and practices often comes from the lessons it teaches us. In the case of Auburn Elementary, teachers' experience of Teacher Lab highlights the necessity of a vibrant professional learning culture for developing and supporting classroom teachers as field-based or associated teacher educators.

Without this rich culture and the professional learning opportunities it provides, Auburn Elementary could not realize its goal of preparing practice-ready teachers who have been coached in what it means to be a life-long learner and leader. In closing, we argue (a) the importance of attending to the learning needs of classroom teachers in order to advance a clinical model of teacher preparation and (b) the value of modeling for preservice teachers the importance of learning across the career.

CLINICAL PREPARATION AND CLASSROOM TEACHERS

Clinical preparation has been described as the "glue" in powerful teacher preparation (Darling-Hammond, 2006). Serving as the bridge between university coursework and school-based teaching, clinical practice plays a critical role in preparing teachers for full-time employment. The importance of field-based experience, as a complement to university-based coursework, is not new. Educational reformers have argued on behalf of increased clinical and/or field-based practice for more than three decades (Ball & Cohen, 1999; Berry, Montgomery, & Snyder, 2008; Cochran-Smith, 1991; Holmes Group, 1990; NCATE, 2010; Thorpe, 2014; Zeichner, 2010).

Conditions considered essential to high-quality learning in the field include carefully selected placements where evidence-based practices in diverse classrooms and under the expert guidance of veteran teachers are common (Darling-Hammond, 2006). In these settings, mentor teachers help preservice candidates develop the stance of a learner through meaningful dialogue based on authentic records of practice and a gradual release of responsibility (Carroll, Featherstone, Featherstone, Feiman-Nemser, & Roosevelt, 2007).

The goal is to provide preservice teachers with authentic opportunities to practice and to reflect on that practice through guided conversation and meaningful feedback (Darling-Hammond & Bransford, 2005). With these conditions as a premise, building the capacity of the educators who work in such settings should be a priority for teacher education programs.

Yet little is known from research about how best to prepare classroom teachers for the role of associated teacher educators—even when we know that classroom teaching is not preparation for mentoring. For example, in a study conducted by Sands and Goodwin (2005), researchers found that elementary teacher mentors lacked proficiency in helping their interns understand mathematics, technology, and the use of academic standards despite working in a school/university partnership.

Dutch researchers have outlined a set of tasks and competencies for teacher educators that might provide a helpful starting point, but their work did not specifically target field-based classroom teachers (Koster, Brekelmans, Korthagen, & Wubbels, 2005). Bullough (2005) suggested that identify formation may serve as a critical turning point for classroom teachers who are adopting the role of teacher educator, but his analysis is based on a single cooperating teacher.

Promising programs designed to train classroom teachers as associated teacher educators are emerging in the literature, but they are largely descriptive and specific to a single program (Norman, 2011; Paulsen, DaFonte, & Barton-Arwood, 2015).

Recognizing their unique status in the teacher education hierarchy, classroom teachers have been described as "boundary spanners" operating in a "hybrid" or "third space" (Zeichner, 2010; see also Bullough, 2005) between school and university. For this critical role, classroom teachers are frequently left to make sense of their responsibilities with little training, limited guidance, and minimal financial support.

It should not be a surprise that teaching practices are more likely to be "caught than taught" in these haphazard settings (Zeichner, 2010). In this project, our purpose was to examine the role that Teacher Lab, as an already-established professional learning practice, might play in supporting the development of classroom teachers as associated teacher educators.

LEARNING FROM THE TEACHER NEXT DOOR

In this chapter, we assert that supportive clinical sites for field-based teacher education are the result of intentional planning, not happenstance. To realize this ambitious vision, however, teacher preparation programs will need to take seriously the learning needs of classroom teachers. We cannot expect classroom teachers to have mastered the understandings and skills needed to coach aspiring teachers in the demands of a complex professional practice. The task of preparing classroom teachers as associated teachers is complicated further by limited human and financial resources.

Even if teacher preparations programs had the resources to provide ongoing opportunities to learn and practice such coaching skills, it is doubtful that school-based practitioners would have the time to add "one more thing" to their already-demanding workloads. For these reasons, we are excited by the potential that school-based job-embedded formats of professional learning offer for clinical teacher preparation.

Through ongoing, sustained, and collaborative professional learning—especially when that learning features live classroom observation and discussion—we believe classroom teachers can acquire the skills needed to work effectively with preservice teachers. We now introduce the Avondale/Oakland University Partnership and its partner school, Auburn Elementary, where teachers regularly "learn from the teacher next door."

Avondale/Oakland University Partnership Mission and Goals

The Avondale/Oakland University partnership was established in 2013 to further the work and mission of both the Avondale School District and Oakland University's School of Education and Human Services. From the beginning, the partnership was envisioned to be a mutually beneficial arrangement that connected local resources and expertise to authentic learning contexts.

As described in a flyer announcing the partnership: "This vision is focused upon teacher preparation, leadership development, social justice, parent and community engagement, and ongoing professional learning opportunities for all staff that can directly lead to improved student academic outcomes."

Today, the Avondale School District serves as a robust clinical site for OU's teacher preparation program by hosting student teachers, mentoring field placement students, and offering on-site methods courses. Additional partnership activities include opportunities for first-year medical students to teach high school students on health topics, for linguistics faculty to run a summer school experience for English language learners, and for health sciences to sponsor a community health fair with free flu shots.

In addition to a close working relationship with the School of Education and Human Services, the partnership has developed relationships with OU's School of Medicine, School of Business, School of Engineering, and the College of Arts and Sciences.

At the center of the partnership is Auburn Elementary, the Avondale/Oakland University Partnership School. As a school of choice, the school draws students from across the district and from neighboring districts to create a culturally, racially, and linguistically diverse population. Dedicated to its mission of becoming a school culture where students are actively engaged in making their thinking visible, Auburn Elementary has spent the past several years implementing a "cultures of thinking" approach to instruction (Ritchhart, 2015; Ritchhart, Church, & Morrison, 2011).

Serving students pre-kindergarten through 5th grade, Auburn is a Title I Targeted Assistance school with 52% of the student population receiving free or reduced lunch. In fall 2013, the school reopened as a partnership school with 17 classroom teachers (9 returning, 5 transfers, and 3 new hires), one teacher leader on special assignment (responsible for coordinating the work of the partnership), and a new building principal. Those applying to work at Auburn did so understanding the district's commitment to working with OU faculty and preservice students through the new partnership.

In addition to its primary educational mission, Auburn Elementary serves as a robust clinical practice site for preservice education students. During fall 2015, three methods classes (with a combined enrollment of 62 students) were held on site; 38 students were completing field placements; 24 students were completing child studies; and six students were preparing for their student teaching assignment.

The Avondale School District, located approximately 21 miles north of Detroit, educates roughly 3,000 students in grades K-12. Nearly 36,000 residents live within the district boundaries, which encompasses portions of four municipalities in Oakland County. The composition of the student population represents a diverse racial population that includes 60% Caucasian, 20% African-American, 11% Asian, and 7% Hispanic. The district is comprised of one high school, one alternative academy (high school), one middle school, and four elementary schools, with 195 full-time teachers on staff.

Teacher Lab at Auburn Elementary

Teacher Lab, a job-embedded approach to professional learning, provides teachers with an opportunity to observe another teacher in action and learn from his or her practice. It is a time for observers to debrief, reflect, and set personal goals for their own practice. It is also a system of collaborative inquiry that supports improved student achievement. As one Auburn teacher noted:

> Our experiences with Teacher Lab help us to fine-tune the dialogue and energy around our professional learning experiences. Through this collaboration, we advance our collective understandings, create a commitment to continuous improvement and strengthen our individual leadership skills. The structure of Teacher Lab learning has accelerated our professional growth and identity development as leaders.

Using a full-day released time format, participating teachers gather to study a pre-selected problem of practice (e.g., close reading of a text) after which they observe teaching of that practice in one or more classrooms. The day ends with a discussion of that same practice with the host teacher. In this way, the group operates much like a PLC that engages in a variety of activities that may include book study, the analysis of student work, and/or the review of data.

While there are numerous variations in the design of a Teacher Lab experience, the typical model includes one facilitating teacher, one host teacher, and 4–10 observing teachers (Oakland Schools, 2014). The development of Teacher Lab in Avondale can be credited to work with a local teacher leadership consultant, who, working through the local intermediate school district to support in-district leadership development, guided Auburn teachers' development of lab learning.

Over time, Teacher Lab has extended throughout the district. The Superintendent's Office provides financial support in the form of substitute teachers. For the 2014/2015 school year, 171 days were utilized for Teacher Lab at a cost of almost $17,000.

Today, Teacher Lab is the preferred format for professional learning, with nearly 94% of district teachers having participated in at least one lab. District teachers frequently describe this model as the most beneficial professional learning they have engaged in. Labs have been designed around new instructional practices and new curriculum. As teachers have come to understand the power of this collaborative structure, labs have also been co-created for targeted educator groups, for example, art teachers and beginning teachers. Since the partnership school opened in 2013, it is not uncommon to find preservice teachers and university faculty working alongside Auburn teachers on lab day, collectively engaged in professional dialogue as partners in learning.

LEARNING TO BE TEACHER EDUCATORS

To demonstrate the power of Teacher Lab for supporting classroom teachers' ongoing learning and development as associated teacher educators, Auburn teachers were invited to share their thoughts on the following questions: (a) In what ways does Teacher Lab support your work with preservice teachers? and (b) What role does Teacher Lab play in nurturing a learning-oriented school culture? Through a series of teacher-written vignettes, we discuss five themes that emerged from these discussions.

The first theme addresses the role of Teacher Lab in helping to nurture a learning community among Auburn teachers. The second theme of noticing, naming, and analyzing the teaching process speaks to the importance of teachers learning how to skillfully decompose and understand constituent parts of the teaching and learning process.

The third theme of giving feedback and coaching highlights the ways in which Teacher Lab helps participating teachers practice giving and receiving meaningful feedback. The fourth theme is that of modeling an inquiry stance toward teaching, which Auburn teachers do through sustained and active participation in Teacher Lab. We end by sharing an additional insight: the role of Teacher Lab in developing classroom teachers' confidence as associated teacher educators.

Becoming a Learning Community

The power of a learning community is well established in the literature (DuFour, Eaker, & DuFour, 2005; Hord, 2008; Stoll & Louis, 2007; Wenger, 1999). Through professional learning communities, teachers are provided an opportunity to talk with one another in authentic and meaningful ways about the teaching and learning process. In the case of Auburn Elementary, Teacher Lab has helped to develop and sustain a professional culture and climate that values an inquiry stance toward teaching practice (Cochran-Smith & Lytle, 2009).

In the two teacher-written vignettes that follow, we see the influence of Teacher Lab on the building of professional culture and community among Auburn teachers: a community that extends to include preservice candidates placed in the building. In the first vignette, we also gain a sense of how Teacher Lab can shift the professional mind-set of an individual teacher.

From Solo Act to Ensemble (Jennifer Johnson, K-5 Music)

Being the only music teacher in the building is a bit of a "solo act." No matter the level of support from other teachers and staff members, there's never an opportunity to run across the hall to share the success or failure of a lesson. After a period of time, you get used to being on your island working, teaching and learning alone. There are occasional opportunities to meet with other teachers of your specialty at meetings or workshops, but nothing like the classroom teachers have. The thought of working with—truly with—another teacher is something that "the others" do. It's a nice opportunity for them, just not for me.

Allowing other teachers, especially other music teachers, into my classroom to see how and what we are learning seemed completely foreign, almost absurd to me. Coming from the music world where we are trained to be in competition with one another (e.g., first chair, soloist), why would or should I share my "tricks of the trade" with those I'm supposed to be in competition with? What if what I'm doing isn't "right" or "good enough"?

For more than a year I watched my colleagues learn and grow through the Teacher Lab experience. They were filled with energy and renewed enthusiasm for their craft. They were encouraging each other to try new things. Rather than hearing "that may work in your room," I heard things like "let me help you make that work for your room" and "let's sit down and talk that through." I've always known that I got my best ideas from watching others, but it was through quiet independent observation, not intentional collaboration. When the idea of a lab for elementary music teachers came up, I was eager to give it a try.

The day of the lab was exciting. The lesson we watched was similar to something that I was trying to work on in my own room. The classroom was like mine with similar equipment and materials. As the day progressed, I felt as though this same thing could happen in my classroom. The teaching and learning I witnessed on that day was inspirational and encouraging.

During our reflection session at the end of the day I realized that I wasn't alone in my thoughts and I didn't feel like I was a solo act any longer. I was part of a learning community. I took the lessons learned back to my classroom to try with my students. More fundamentally, I gained confidence as a learner and teacher.

The experience of Teacher Lab has made the idea of a learning community real for me. I am no longer just delivering the curriculum to the students. Everyone in the room, no matter the grade or age, is a learner. This mindset has made an incredible difference in my teaching. Because of Teacher Lab, I am better able to answer questions from students, administration, parents and especially pre-service teachers.

The questions pre-service teachers ask are unlike those of others who come into my room. Pre-service teachers are interested in the how and why of what I am teaching. Because of Teacher Lab, I am more comfortable having "grown-ups" in my classroom, more confident in my teaching and better prepared to answer questions asked by pre-service teachers.

We believe Jennifer's story of reluctance and fear is common among teachers. When teachers take the risk to collaborate and interact equally as partners in learning, however, good things can happen. Working in partnership with one another is as much about shared learning as it is about shared power. Imagine the opportunities that are lost as teachers work within a school culture that breeds competition, where wearing the crown as the "most requested" teacher is deemed more desirable than being known as the "most collegial."

Today, as Auburn's school culture welcomes new members into its learning community, intentional decisions are made that nurture relationships and facilitate partnerships among all teachers, both in-service and preservice. This commitment to being inclusive is particularly evident in the next vignette.

Our Community Grows (Colleen Bugaj, Kindergarten)

A new school year always brings a sense of anticipation. New students, new routines, new learning and . . . a student teacher! I prepared for her arrival by acquiring a new desk from the storeroom (which I pushed up against mine), selected some favorite resource books to share and selected a cute journal that would serve as a form of communication between us. That completed, I reflected on how to make this experience successful. Remembering previous student teachers, I knew that our days together would be a balance of modeling, reflecting, discussion and observation.

Using Teacher Lab as my model, I will commit to modeling my teaching practice so that my student teacher may begin to develop her own classroom practice. Like the conversation among colleagues that is so vital to Teacher Lab, ongoing reflection and dialogue will be vital to our relationship.

And, just as being deliberate and specific in giving feedback is critical in Teacher Lab, I will commit to mindfully sharing observations of my student teacher's practice. I will thank her for her efforts, talk her through challenges and model for her the vulnerability and openness that I wish from myself and my colleagues (Brown, 2012). And since relationships are key to why Teacher Lab works, I will work hard to ground our work in trust and honesty.

As Colleen concludes, "I am reminded again how valuable Teacher Lab has been to me as I improve my own teaching practice. I also now see its value as a structure for ensuring the success of this young teacher." Welcoming the next generation of professionals to the table can be a daunting task.

Through Teacher Lab, Auburn teachers are learning how to partner with preservice teachers in the classrooms and also how to establish strong lines of communication so as to facilitate reflective dialogue. Relationships *are* key. As open and reflective dialogue is modeled, practiced, and nurtured within the wider professional community, a strong foundation of trust can be created.

Noticing, Naming, and Analyzing the Teaching/Learning Process

One of the skill sets that Auburn teachers acquire from participating in Teacher Lab and observing live instruction is that of noticing, naming, and analyzing the teaching and learning process. It is widely documented that classroom teachers may be highly skilled in their respective areas of expertise, yet their understandings of teaching remain largely tacit, for example, why concepts and skills are taught in a particular order, why some student questions prompt elaborate teacher responses and others yield barely a nod (Freeman, 1991; Schon, 1987).

When a preservice teacher asks why something is done in a particular way, classroom teachers may find themselves at a loss for words. Importantly, Teacher Lab provides teachers with the opportunity to closely observe live teaching and then "think out loud" (Feiman-Nemser & Buchmann, 1987) as they reflect together on the observation. As a result, building teachers begin to develop a shared language around instructional practice. They gain practice in unpacking teaching strategies, as well as supporting the learning process for students. They also have opportunities to make sense of what they see, including the identification of new or revised teaching moves. The following vignettes provide illustrations of this skill building.

Developing a Shared Language (Serena Stock, 2nd Grade)

As a Teacher Lab host my experience has been equal parts energizing and nerve racking. Opening up one's classroom can be intimidating! For example, a few years ago I attended a powerful Visible Thinking seminar with Ron Ritchhart and was eager to implement a series of "thinking routines" in my classroom (Ritchhart et al., 2011).

I shared this excitement with my colleagues, who expressed interest in following my journey of implementing these new instructional strategies through Teacher Lab. In the past I would have been apprehensive. After being involved in Teacher Lab for multiple years, however, I was up for the challenge.

During the course of that year I was able to share with colleagues how a thinking culture grew in my classroom (Ritchhart, 2015). Through observation, colleagues witnessed my personal victories, frustrations and occasional defeats. These teaching situations were authentic and the feedback I received was critical. Through the thought provoking questions of my colleagues, I found myself becoming more and more reflective.

In turn, answering the "whys" of teaching became easier. My responses became more readily accessible and authentic as I became more reflective. Together we were developing a shared vocabulary: a language of learning. Through post-observation work, I continued to develop my skills as we shared articles, websites, books, and videos to strengthen our teaching. The ability to collaborate with others in such a positive and affirming way was a gift that I carry to this day.

As teachers strive to manage student learning challenges and incorporate new instructional strategies amid the demands of an ever-changing educational landscape, they need dedicated time to create shared meaning and a deep sense of understanding. Through the lab experience, teachers are able to unpack these demands and challenges together. Through facilitated conversation, they have the opportunity to validate the elements of instruction and pedagogy that are familiar and make connections to new or unknown information with confidence.

Together, they develop a shared language around shared instructional practices. Teachers working in an environment that supports Teacher Lab or other job-embedded professional learning models are able to enact their new learning more confidently, knowing that a supportive network—a safety net—is readily available, right next door. In the next vignette, early career teacher Molly draws on this new vocabulary to practice noticing and naming teaching practices with both her teaching colleagues and her preservice students.

Noticing and Naming Purposeful Practice (Molly Abbott, 1st Grade)

I observed many teachers during my field placements as an Oakland University student and not one was able to explain why they do what they do with as much purpose and direction as my Auburn colleagues. I have met and worked with teachers who would explain their lessons as something they have, well, just always done. They rarely elaborated on why they chose to respond to one student differently than another, or how a student's interjection may or may not have changed the entire course of the lesson. My first experience with Teacher Lab proved to me that Auburn teachers approach their work and learning quite differently.

In my first experience with lab learning I observed a colleague working with a guided reading group. The students were doing a thinking routine using words from the text to identify word patterns. While our goal was to observe instruction through the lens of visible thinking routines, I came away learning so much more. For example, our post-observation discussion made it clear that the text choice was purposeful and the word list intentionally selected.

I quickly realized that the lesson was developed and planned around the individual needs of students in the observed reading group, and not a preplanned lesson that doesn't change from one year or group to another. At the time, this powerful observation prompted further conversation with this colleague about age-appropriate strategies for individualizing instruction.

For me, the value in Teacher Lab comes from the opportunity to speak about teaching by analyzing teaching with other teachers. The insights I have learned from this process have been so valuable in my conversations with pre-service teachers. Even with my limited teaching experience, I am able to clearly express the purpose and direction behind each lesson.

I now answer questions from pre-service teachers about why I do what I do in my classroom, and I share the experiences I have had or have observed, that lead me to draw conclusions about what works best for me and my classroom.

While many teachers are eager to collaborate, they don't always have the skills necessary to facilitate collaborative conversations with their colleagues. Moreover, the time that is so precious and vital to learning is often lost during team meetings and loosely structured PLC groups. Teachers may also struggle to name the understandings and beliefs that drive their decision making in the classroom.

In short, they haven't yet acquired an awareness of the need to make the tacit explicit (Freeman, 1991). This is one of the primary benefits of Teacher Lab for classroom teachers as associated teacher educators. Through lab learning teachers develop a shared vocabulary for talking about teaching and learning. They also acquire the skills needed for making visible their teaching decisions.

Giving Feedback and Coaching Others Toward Improved Practice

A complementary skill gained through Teacher Lab is the process of giving and receiving feedback for instructional improvement. This is especially important given that we work in a profession with established norms of privacy, autonomy, and egalitarianism (Little, 1982; Lortie, 1975). Lab learning helps teachers de-privatize teaching in ways that help them get better at teaching. Through Teacher Lab, teachers learn to give feedback and coach with care and intention.

In turn, this intentionality helps to build the trust that supports learning. In the following vignette, Molly explains how Teacher Lab has helped her transition from giving generic advice to giving honest and targeted feedback that is teacher and classroom specific.

From Advice to Meaningful Feedback (Molly Abbott, 1st Grade)

As a participant in Teacher Lab, I am always so appreciative of the teachers who host us in their classrooms. One way that we share our appreciation is through meaningful feedback. We never say a simple, "Good job. I liked it." The host teacher deserves more than an easy compliment. While it may be true, we know as educators that a simple "good job" doesn't help anyone grow.

The words we use are carefully and deliberately chosen to provide the host with a sense of deep appreciation for her work, along with a specific comment or observation designed to help her reflect and grow. It's no easy task to allow four or more adults watch you teach (highly distractible) children. The feedback that we provide our colleagues builds a trusting environment where teachers feel safe offering to host future labs.

Understanding the purpose and importance of feedback via Teacher Lab has especially helped me while working with Oakland University pre-service teachers. So many Oakland University students are placed with classroom teachers who are indifferent to their learning and who give universally high evaluations at the completion of their placement. Their feedback is often more akin to advice giving. In my classroom, pre-service teachers are held to high expectations and are given honest, specific feedback based on their performance.

Giving meaningful and truthful feedback is an art that teachers can struggle to master. In Molly's vignette, we see how Teacher Lab helped her to learn, largely through observation and experience, the importance of giving and receiving honest and specific feedback. As an early career teacher who works with field-placement students, this awareness has been critical to her preparation and readiness as an associated teacher educator. In the next vignette, Colleen describes how purposeful conversations about teaching and learning are the "new normal" at Auburn Elementary.

Talking About Teaching: A New Normal (Colleen Bugaj, Kindergarten)

Flush with nerves and excitement, I entered the conference room and sat at the table with some of my dearest friends and closest colleagues. We had just completed a classroom observation of my kindergarteners participating in writers' workshop. The classroom observation went well and the conversation that followed remains one of my most cherished memories as an educator.

My colleagues were generous with their praise, eager to ask questions and generally delighted to have uninterrupted time to discuss our daily teaching practice. Admittedly, the approval from these fellow educators meant a great deal to me. As I listened to the questions about my practice and attempted to articulate my reasons for particular choices I felt a new strength as a teacher.

Today, Teacher Lab has created a new normal at our school. This normal includes hosting small groups of colleagues who meet to observe our teaching and then later discuss the modeled teaching practice. Our normal allows us to look closely at the practice of a teacher and encourages us to participate in a discussion of that practice.

This normal allows teachers to become involved in the practice of a colleague and to mentor in ways we never could when we taught with our door shut. Our normal has grown to include giving and receiving meaningful feedback to others, while also providing an opportunity to use that feedback ourselves.

Through lab learning teachers are offered a coveted front row seat, a view into another educator's practice. As trust is established within the school culture and feedback from colleagues is encouraged and expected, each participant, regardless of the role he or she plays within the culture, is reminded that every educator is a teacher and a learner. Regardless of experience or credentials listed on a resume, opportunities are given and authentic feedback is offered.

As a result, the conversation within this school culture becomes rich with the sharing of new ideas, concepts, and instructional strategies. Viewed this way, Teacher Lab does more than develop coaching skills in classroom teachers; Teacher Lab also facilitates and nurtures a way of professional being in the building.

Modeling an Inquiry Stance

By including preservice teachers in Teacher Lab, Auburn teachers are modeling a structured process for working collaboratively with other teachers to improve practice. Through participation in Teacher Lab, they are further modeling an inquiry stance toward continuous improvement (Cochran-Smith & Lytle, 2009). Given the university's limited resources for supporting classroom teachers as associated teacher educators, Teacher Lab fills a critical gap by equipping classroom teachers with mentoring skills, while also supporting a building culture that honors learning through inquiry. The next vignette by veteran teacher Serena illustrates how preservice teachers are naturally invited into the inquiry process.

Teach, Learn, Model, Repeat (Serena Stock, 2nd Grade)

I had a student teacher the same year I hosted a series of Teacher Labs which all focused on my efforts to establish a culture of thinking in my classroom

(Ritchhart, 2015). *This student teacher experienced lab for the first time when teachers came in to observe a thinking routine called Generate, Sort, Connect (Ritchhart et al., 2011).*

She, along with the group, watched as the visibility of students' thinking slowly and surely began to form across the year. She also saw me being observed and experienced the feedback and collaboration that followed.

During her time in my classroom, I made sure that my student teacher was fully involved in the creation of a culture of thinking in our classroom. As a result of her involvement in previous labs, she had the confidence to take a more active role in our final lab that year.

At the end of the day, during our final hosting, she shared visible thinking lessons and activities that she had completed during her student teaching, including the use of thinking routines to teach an entire social studies unit. She shared what visible thinking meant to her and how she would develop and use the strategies in her future classroom. She relished the feedback as it was shared in a safe place full of collaborative support.

Preservice teachers are often relegated to a back seat when participating in school-based professional development opportunities. At Auburn Elementary the opposite is true. Teacher Lab is purposefully designed to be welcoming and nurturing for all teachers, regardless of experience. In Serena's example, we see the power of this welcoming stance as her student teacher assumes a leadership role in the final Teacher Lab of the year. Similarly, Sarah's vignette that follows captures the reaction of a pre-service teacher to being included in the routine professional conversations about teaching and learning that are so common in the building's collaborative environment.

This Really Happens? (Sarah Bruha, 2nd Grade)

I can remember an occasion where one of my field placement teachers was able to witness the fruits of our collaborative labor first-hand. It was common planning time and my teaching partner and I were discussing how to introduce interactive science notebooks to our second graders. I invited my pre-service teacher to observe during our impromptu conversation.

Because my teaching partner and I had collaborated together during many Teacher Lab experiences, the conversation was genuine and collegial in nature. We spent the next fifteen minutes or so trouble-shooting our approach to rolling out notebooks in class.

When we got up to leave, my pre-service teacher stopped us and said, "Wait . . . this type of thing really happens? You two actually sit down and collaborate with one another on a daily basis? I hear about it from my professors and read about in my course books, but I have never actually seen this type of collaboration in real life."

At that moment I realized that perhaps this type of authentic and meaningful conversation does not always happen in schools and that pre-service teachers may have few opportunities to witness this type of collaboration for themselves. This experience solidified—not only for myself, but also for my field placement student—that teaching is not just about learning how to teach, it is also about collaborating and growing yourself in order to impact your students in a positive way.

As we see in this vignette, job-embedded professional learning that is collaborative, sustained, and inquiry-driven can play a powerful role in supporting all teachers' learning, from the veteran, to the new, to the prospective. Moreover, the opportunity to witness and participate in powerful and relevant professional learning in the field increases the likelihood that preservice teachers will enter the profession expecting a collaborative learning-oriented work environment.

Developing Confidence as Associated Teacher Educators

Finally, Teacher Lab has built teachers' confidence: a confidence that shines through the vignettes that have been shared. Through live observations of teaching, teachers better understand their instructional practice. They develop trusting relationships with their colleagues, and they learn to talk in depth about the teaching and learning processes.

While this learning has been important to all Auburn teachers, it has particular importance for the newest members of the staff who are tasked with supporting prospective teacher learning and still themselves learning to teach (Feiman-Nemser, 2001). The following vignettes, by early career teachers Molly and Sarah, uniquely capture the significance of this experience.

Forever Changed (Molly Abbott, 1st Grade)

I am a very reflective person, which I think originated in my lack of confidence as a new teacher in the building. I was always considering, "Is there a way that I could have done that better?" Taking part in Teacher Lab has enhanced my self-reflective nature and given me the confidence to speak about my teaching with peers, veteran teachers, administrators and pre-service teachers.

When I began teaching, I didn't feel that I had much to offer seasoned teachers because I was still learning so much. Lab nurtured my confidence and growth, so that now I can (without too much apprehension) keep my doors open to all learners in our building, from pre-service teachers and colleagues to parents, administrators and university faculty members. Teacher Lab is incredibly powerful for teachers like me who are always reflecting to improve. I will never view professional development the same again!

Our nations' schools are full of teachers like Molly and Sarah, early career teachers who want to grow and develop throughout their career. Uniquely, Teacher Lab offers such teachers a standards-based learning format and structure that is job-embedded, inquiry-driven, collaborative, and sustained (Learning Forward, 2011). Over time, this approach to professional learning builds instructional expertise and confidence in participants. It also supports their capacity to support preservice teachers.

Learning What It Means to Be a Teacher (Sarah Bruha, 2nd Grade)

Even though I was in the early stages of my career, the choice to open my doors to pre-service teachers from Oakland University came easily. Some new or beginning teachers might have felt they had little to offer pre-service teachers because of their inexperience. Because of the collaborative nature of our school culture and the inquiry-based approach of my experience in Teacher Lab, however, I felt secure in opening my doors to these pre-service teachers.

I felt confident in knowing that everyone has something to contribute and everyone can engage in the learning process.

In my interactions with my field placement students I am usually bursting at the seams to discuss and share my Teacher Lab experiences. This offers me a chance to not only share the impactful and authentic learning that happens during Teacher Lab, but it also opens doors for further conversations about what it means to be a teacher and how to improve our craft as educators for the betterment of all learners, child and adult alike.

My collaboration and listening skills have improved through Teacher Lab, allowing me to both connect and collaborate with pre-service teachers. I am able to model lifelong learning, which would not be possible without my active participation in Teacher Lab and the inquiry-based environment that is cultivated in our school community.

The ongoing learning needs of teachers are paramount, are critically important, and should be attended to closely. As we work with preservice teachers, it is crucial that we design and nurture authentic cultures and systems that nurture opportunities for continuous growth and reflection. The promise of designing professional learning environments that engage teachers in ongoing professional learning not only sustains teachers, as these vignettes so powerfully demonstrate, but also provides a pathway of understanding for preservice teachers.

IMPLICATIONS FOR FIELD-BASED TEACHER EDUCATION

Lev Vygotsky (1978) teaches us that children grow into the intellectual life around them. At Auburn Elementary, teachers have increasingly found themselves substituting the word "teachers" for children. Regardless of one's role in lab learning, the opportunities for professional learning abound. As Serena notes,

> Experiencing teaching and learning first hand, through Teacher Lab, is powerful. I am exposed to new teaching strategies.
>
> I notice things that are familiar and make connections that enable me to name new understandings that I can take back to my classroom and use right away. I recognize similarities that will draw us closer together collegially. I notice, with awe, the strengths of the educators that surround me; strengths that are often unknown to me before observing their classroom. I discover and realize the talents of those who I can now call upon in the spirit of collaboration. Long story short, I am energized by Teacher Lab.

Set within a robust school/university partnership context, classroom teachers are not the only ones who benefit from lab learning. Preservice teachers at Auburn Elementary are welcomed as full participants in the Teacher Lab community. In this final vignette, Marcia recounts the story of Melissa, a field placement student preparing to student teach in the building.

I Am, Because You Are (Marcia Hudson, Lead Teacher Leader)

As a slight blush blossoms across her face, Melissa continues: "I remember teaching one of my first lessons at Auburn . . . and it wasn't going well. I realized that I didn't possess the classroom management skills that I thought I had. I didn't have the attention of the students. I wanted to cry. I wanted to yell. I was frustrated because I couldn't do what I wanted to do. I got through the lesson and was quite thrown by the experience." Melissa's face clouds over momentarily with the memory.

Quickly brightening, she adds, "As the students left the room for recess, the cooperating teacher asked if I would like to talk. I was embarrassed, but welcomed the chance to debrief. After asking me about my overall thoughts, she told me what she had observed, what these observations made her think about, and asked me questions that helped me think about the experience more critically.

Even though our conversation was only about ten minutes long, I left the classroom with a deeper understanding about teaching and learning than I had ever had before. Getting this kind of feedback gave me a chance to reflect on what I had done well, think about what I could do better and become aware of things that I had never considered. It was invaluable. It was so much more meaningful to me than "that was great." The next time I taught, the lesson went better. I was able to redeem myself."

Melissa's next comment shows that she further understands the importance of professional collaboration and continuous improvement. "After working through that sense of failure, and talking about my lesson with another teacher, I think that I learned something even more valuable.

I learned that every lesson isn't going to go perfectly and it's okay to share your concerns with others. It's okay to be vulnerable and think through your failures with others around you. You are not going to be perfect every time. It's okay to open yourself up to critique and suggestions. It made me truly appreciate the opportunity that I had to work in a school that valued and modeled this kind of open, collaborative, reflective practice."

Melissa's story is a testament to the power of Teacher Lab as a job-embedded format for professional learning. Inquiry-driven at the core, sustained over time, and highly collaborative, Teacher Lab authentically connects to teachers' daily work and easily adapts for all stages of the career. We see this vividly in Melissa's account, continued here.

At Auburn, every teacher's door is opened. I can walk through the hallways and stop and ask any teacher in the school a question. I am invited to come into their classrooms. If several are talking in a small group, and I approach them, they never stop talking, but just take a step back and include me in the circle of conversation . . . It's like I am this little seed . . . and many of them are like the bees, buzzing around me, helping to pollinate and encourage my growth. This is an environment that helps me blossom. This kind of guidance is priceless.

As we argue in this chapter, preservice teachers deserve strong mentoring that includes meaningful and targeted feedback. Moreover, preservice teachers should have the opportunity to experience the power of a positive learning–focused professional community. Teacher Lab, as we have illustrated through teachers' personal reflections, offers both.

As teacher educators, we hope all of our preservice teachers will have an experience as rich as Melissa describes; we wish for this knowing that we have few dedicated resources and little authority for the school settings in which we place our students. This is precisely why we find the Teacher Lab model so promising. The case of Auburn Elementary provides an exemplar from which we can learn how existing forms of job-embedded professional learning provide a context in which classroom teachers, as associated teacher educators, can develop their practice as mentors and coaches.

CONCLUSION

Colleen summarized for us the value of Teacher Lab when she wrote:

Teacher Lab began with the vision of several teachers who looked to develop an authentic learning experience for the teachers at our school, using the knowledge and talent of the teachers that teach every day in our building. It makes a powerful statement to recognize that strong research-based practices, modeled in an authentic setting, can be the basis for our professional learning.

Inviting pre-service teachers into the classroom to be mentored by our staff is a natural and logical next step.

Through the support of the central office, teachers in Avondale have regular opportunities to build their understanding of the needs of adult learners and of the conditions necessary for effective professional learning through Teacher Lab. In turn, this learning serves as a foundation for supporting the development of preservice teachers and, by association, their field-based mentors as teacher educators.

Although the relationship between Teacher Lab and preservice teacher development has yet to be tested empirically, we are encouraged by what we observe and hear from Oakland University students completing field placements in the building. Preservice teachers placed at Auburn are experiencing genuine professional collaboration and community as they work side by side with teachers who model inquiry and lifelong learning. As an added bonus, Teacher Lab ensures that newer teachers like Molly and Sarah are better equipped, early in their career, to assist in the mentoring of prospective teachers. Preservice candidate Melissa is not alone in hoping she finds a school like Auburn when she graduates.

As the field extends and enhances the clinical component of teacher education, we hope program directors will look to job-embedded forms of professional learning—particularly those that feature observation and discussion of live instruction—as legitimate sites for teachers' learning as associated teacher educators.

When veteran teachers are willing to be vulnerable in front of their colleagues, they provide a powerful model for prospective teachers to emulate. We further hope that program directors strive to cultivate field placement sites that support job-embedded forms of professional learning like Teacher Lab. As the case of Auburn Elementary illustrates, context matters.

Further research is needed that explores the relationship between job-embedded professional learning and the development of classroom teachers as associated teacher educators. Nonetheless, this test case highlights the potential link that exists between the two. Without Teacher Lab, Auburn teachers would still be performing as solo acts. Instead, lab learning has provided teachers at all stages of the career—from prospective to veteran—an opportunity to live into a truly professional way of being.

REFERENCES

Ball, D. L., & Cohen, D. K. (1999). Developing practice; developing practitioners: Toward a practice-based theory of professional education. In L. Darling-Hammond & G. Sykes (Eds.), *Teaching as a learning profession: Handbook of policy and practice* (pp. 3–32). San Francisco, CA: Jossey-Bass.

Berry, B., Montgomery, D., & Snyder, J. (2008). *Urban teacher residency models and institutes of higher education: Implications for teacher preparation.* Washington, DC: NCATE.

Brown, B. (2012). *Daring greatly. How the courage to be vulnerable transforms the way we live, love, parent, and lead.* New York, NY: Gotham Books.

Bullough, R. V. (2005). Being and becoming a mentor: School-based teacher educators and teacher educator identity. *Teaching and Teacher Education, 21*, 143–155.

Carroll, D., Featherstone, H., Featherstone, J., Feiman-Nemser, S., & Roosevelt, D. (2007). *Transforming teacher education: Reflections from the field.* Cambridge, MA: Harvard University Press.

Cochran-Smith, M. (1991). Reinventing student teaching. *Journal of Teacher Education, 42*, 104–118.

Cochran-Smith, M., & Lytle, S. L. (2009). *Inquiry as stance: Practitioner research for the next generation.* New York, NY: Teachers College.

Darling-Hammond, L. (2006). *Powerful teacher education: Lessons from exemplary programs.* San Francisco, CA: Jossey-Bass.

Darling-Hammond, L., & Bransford, D. (2005). *Preparing teachers for a changing world: What teachers should learn and be able to do.* San Francisco, CA: Jossey-Bass.

DuFour, R., Eaker, R., & DuFour, R. (2005). *On common ground: The power of professional learning communities.* Bloomington, IN: Solution Tree.

Feiman-Nemser, S. (2001). From preparation to practice: Designing a continuum to strengthen and sustain teaching. *Teachers College Record, 103*(6), 1013–1055.

Feiman-Nemser, S., & Buchmann, M. (1987). When is student teaching teacher education? *Teaching and Teacher Education, 3*, 255–273.

Freeman, D. (1991). "To make the tacit explicit": Teacher education, emerging discourse, and conceptions of teaching. *Teaching and Teacher Education, 7*(5–6), 439–454.

Holmes Group (1990). *Tomorrow's schools: Principles for the design of professional development schools.* East Lansing, MI: Author.

Hord, S. M. (2008). Evolution of the professional learning community: Revolutionary concept is based on intentional collegial learning. *Journal of Staff Development, 29*(3), 10–13.

Koster, B., Brekelmans, M., Korthagen, F., & Wubbels, T. (2005). Quality requirements for teacher educators. *Teaching and Teacher Education, 21*, 157–176.

Learning Forward. (2011). *Standards for professional learning.* Oxford, OH: Author.

Little, J. W. (1982). Norms of collegiality and experimentation: Workplace conditions of school success. *American Educational Research Journal, 19*(3), 325–340.

Lortie, D. C. (1975). *Schoolteacher: A sociological study.* Chicago, IL: University of Chicago Press.

National Council for the Accreditation of Teacher Education. (2010). *Standards for professional development schools.* Washington, DC: Author.

Norman, P. J. (2011). Planning for what kind of teaching? Supporting cooperating teachers as teachers of planning. *Teacher Education Quarterly, 38*(3), 49–68.

Oakland Schools. (2014). *Job-embedded professional learning: Creating by and for teachers in Oakland County, Michigan.* Retrieved from http://tinyurl.com/jxsjc2n

Paulsen, K., DaFonte, A., & Barton-Arwood, S. (2015). The role of mentors in developing and implementing high-quality field-based placements. *Intervention in School and Clinic, 51*(2), 97–105.

Ritchhart, R. (2015). *Creating cultures of thinking: The 8 forces we must master to truly transform our schools*. San Francisco, CA: Jossey-Bass.

Ritchhart, R., Church, M., & Morrison, K. (2011). *Making thinking visible: How to promote engagement, understanding, and independence for all learners*. San Francisco, CA: Jossey-Bass.

Sands, D. I., & Goodwin, L. D. (2005). Shared responsibility for teacher preparation: An exploratory study of the match between skills of clinical teachers and those required of their teacher candidates. *Teaching and Teacher Education, 21*, 817–828.

Schon, D. (1987). *Educating the reflective practitioner*. San Francisco, CA: Jossey-Bass.

Stoll, L., & Louis, K. S. (2007). *Professional learning communities: Divergence, depth and dilemmas*. New York, NY: Open University Press.

Thorpe, R. (2014). Residency: Can it transform teaching the way it did medicine? *Phi Delta Kappa, 96*(1), 36–40.

Vygotsky, L. S. (1978*). Mind in society: The development of higher mental process*. Cambridge, MA: Harvard University Press.

Wenger, E. (1999). *Communities of practice: Learning, meaning and identity*. New York, NY: Cambridge University Press.

Zeichner, K. (2010). Rethinking the connections between campus courses and field experiences in college- and university-based teacher education. *Journal of Teacher Education, 61*(1–2), 89–99.

Chapter 4

Promoting ATE Standards for Professional Development in Pre-K Settings

Noran L. Moffett, Melanie M. Frizzell, Yolanda Brownlee-Williams, Stacye A. Blount, and Nurah-Talibah N. Moffett

ABSTRACT

The purpose of this mixed-methods case study was to examine the impact of ATE Standards on 38 pre-kindergarten educators (PKE) in several rural sites in state and/or federally funded preschool programs in Southeastern classrooms. The findings suggested that it is paramount for educators and administrators in Pre-K classrooms housed within private agencies and faith-based centers to promote effective systematic professional development. Most glaringly for the future of the children, it is recommended that ATE Standard 3 (ATE, n.d.) be conceptualized at the very basic level of human understanding by all care-givers of young children.

KEYWORDS

classroom, Head Start, instructional coach, pre-kindergarten, pre-kindergarten experience, private agency, professional development, rural setting, teacher observation, teaching experience

In the United States, free public education is available for children who are eligible to enroll in grades K-12. Eligibility for traditional public schools is determined through neighborhood zoning, and all children are eligible for a free public school education. However, in some states, particularly in the South, pre-kindergarten is not available free of charge, despite its proven importance. In fact, Dove (2015) contended that "long before we turn our children over to the educational system, we should begin to lay the groundwork that will prepare them to take full advantage of the learning process" (p. 160).

Practice and common sense also supports theoretical claims. During his February 2013 State of the Union Address, President Obama stressed the importance of providing free high-quality preschool available throughout the country so it would broaden the chances of academic success for children, particularly for those who need the most—less advantaged children (Remarks by the President in the State of the Union Address, 2013, The Atlantic, 2013).

There is empirical research supporting the president's claim. The call to increase early childhood education lies in the fact that it provides young children (less than 5 years of age) the opportunity to learn basic academic skills that will not only prepare them for kindergarten but may also increase children's long-term academic knowledge, graduation rates, and the ability to find employment (e.g., Barnett, Carolan, Squires, Clarke Brown, & Chapman, 2014; Kamerman & Gatenio-Gabel, 2007).

Defining what high-quality preschool education means for every child remains a challenge. Research claims that high-quality preschool education means that every teacher responsible for educating young children possess at the minimum a child development associate's degree (Kamerman & Gatenio-Gabel, 2007). Nevertheless, regardless of the numerous facets of high-quality education for young children around the country, it is paramount that all children have the opportunity to begin on equal levels and that this education is provided by qualified personnel who possess early education qualifications, in forms of a license and/or an early childhood education degree.

HISTORY OF EARLY CHILDHOOD EDUCATION: A GLOBAL PERSPECTIVE

Convinced that a prevailing republic needed a literate society, Massachusetts passed the first Public School Act in 1647 (Dove, 2015). In 1698, the charity school movement in England was an early attempt to educate children from poor families (Cahan, 1989). In fact, Cahan indicated that "infant schools began to appear in Great Britain and Europe in the early 19th century" with advocates contending the schools would prevent crime and juvenile delinquency while others hoped it would serve as social reform (p. 9).

In 1787, Thomas Jefferson proposed an educational system to the Virginia legislature consisting of 3 years of public school to all white children of the commonwealth with only the smartest male students being enrolled in grammar school and then college at the expense of the public (Anderson, 1988). Many factors led to the creation of child-care facilities, including the need to provide options for children whose mothers worked outside the home (Cahan, 1989; Kamerman & Gatenio-Gabel, 2007).

In 1965, in an effort to combat the educational inequalities of children from low socioeconomic households, the federal funded program, Head Start, was developed to provide educational and parental support to low-income families. According to Kamerman and Gatenio-Gabel (2007), the Head Start program was designed to target less advantaged children. The authors indicated that its core goals include serving 3–4-year-olds, as well as "comprehensive education, health, nutrition, social and other services" (Kamerman & Gatenio-Gabel, 2007, p. 24).

Despite its importance, in the same year, "only eighteen states in the U.S. funded public kindergarten; by 1970, eighty percent of five year olds attended public kindergarten and, in 2000, all states funded some sort of universal kindergarten program" (Kamerman & Gatenio-Gabel, 2007, p. 24). Public pre-kindergarten education was funded by at least 28 states by the year 1998. Beginning in 1995, Georgia implemented a universal program available to all eligible 4-year-old children in the state (Georgia Department of Early Care and Learning, 2015; Barnett et al., 2014).

In the 21st century, and more than a half century after the recognition of the importance of public pre-kindergarten, North Carolina remains five decades behind. Most recently Barnett and colleagues (2014) defined a state-funded preschool program as grounded in the following seven principles. These programs usually serve children of preschool age consisting of ages 3 and 4. Barnett and colleagues (2014) contended that early childhood education is the primary focus of the program, not parent education, and that group learning experience is offered to the children at least 2 days per week.

They also indicated that distinct from the state's system for subsidized child care but may be coordinated and integrated with the subsidy system for child care, and are not primarily designed to serve children with disabilities although services may be offered to children with disabilities (Barnett et al., 2014). Lastly, they explained that state supplements to the federal Head Start program are considered to constitute state preschool programs if they substantially expand the number of children served, and if the state assumes some administrative responsibility for the program (Barnett et al., 2014).

A HOLISTIC VIEW OF THE EDUCATORS' PROFESSION AND PROFESSIONAL DEVELOPMENT

For educators of young children, one of the best parts of teaching is to see how students absorb knowledge in their early years. Educators who work with young children often display committed and enthusiastic behavior as they teach young children how to learn through play and apply critical-thinking skills. In fact, Adler (1982) explained, "There are no unteachable children. There are only schools and teachers and parents who fail to teach them" (p. 8).

Roosevelt (2011) eloquently indicated that the teacher's profession has moved away from its primary purpose to "help children learn" to a capitalist business model where "teachers are generally expected to be capable "managers" and are supposed to "add value" to students by "teaching to the standards" (p. 242). However, this business model is broken, because it does not offer the proper support for these educators to thrive in this new context.

It is well known that K-12 educators need professional development, particularly in their first years in the profession (Avalos, 2011). It should be no different for educators teaching children birth through 5 years old. These educators are building a foundation for children developmental learning, and they need continued support throughout their first years of teaching. Perhaps one of the most challenging parts of teaching young children is developing a classroom management system grounded on professional development that not only works for the children but the educators as well.

Teaching pre-kindergarten children may be challenging as it employs the educator to consistently be aware of the children as well as develop interactive activities based on projected student outcomes. This can be accomplished only by continuous professional development of the educator, especially those new to the profession.

According to a pearl of wisdom from Dr. Pearlie C. Dove, "We need to put aside our differences in the struggle for control of and on whose turf professional growth should occur. The overriding issue is to create the most favorable teaching/learning environment for lifelong learning." (Moffett & Dove, 2015, p. 84).

Consequently, selected studies of innovation suggest that sustained improvement in teaching often hinges on the development of "teachers as learners" who collaborate with one another to study teaching and its effects (Blase & Blase, 2004, p. 65).

Pre-kindergarten educators, particularly those whose are teaching 4-year-old children for the first time, may greatly benefit from training and professional development that focus on developmentally appropriate practices, lesson plan development, assessment, and an overall introduction into the pre-kindergarten

(PK) day. These trainings provide opportunities for educators to collaborate with other novice and veteran pre-k educators, gain new and innovative teaching tools, and ask presenters (coaches or former coaches) questions in an open forum. It is suggested that the framework that describes how educators are motivated to accomplish goals by their directors and/or principals can be viewed through the lens of path-goal theory (Northhouse, 2010). Continually, "the challenge is to use a leadership style that best meets subordinates' motivational needs . . . by choosing behaviors that complement or supplement what is missing in the work setting" (Northhouse, 2010, p. 125).

Meaningful and culturally appropriated professional and leadership development is much needed in this arena and needs to be prioritized. Research suggests that often low-income students are taught by educators who not only lack the knowledge and understanding of urban students but are also less qualified and prepared than educators serving in middle- to high-income school districts (e.g., Darling-Hammond, 2010; Ladson-Billings, 2009). According to Hill, Friedland and Phelps (2012), pre-Kindergarten student populations are becoming more diverse but the majority of educators are predominantly white middle-class individuals who often speak only one language.

In order for educators, particularly first-year PKEs, to develop an appreciation of the children and families they serve, programs may need to implement more than just a discussion of diversity, but also a way to put culturally relevant teaching into practice. "Defining what constitutes cultural competence in new teachers and identifying how teacher education programs help teachers develop cultural competency receive much attention in the field" (Dee, 2012, p. 263).

Hence, it is perceived that teacher preparation programs may need to extend the capacity of preservice candidates for classroom and clinical experiences to support children who predominantly are from low SES backgrounds and to support diversity and cultural understanding (Dee, 2012; del Prado Hill, Friedland & Phelps, 2012).

Although novice educators may enter their programs with preconceived ideologies about children of color, the exposure to numerous cultural awareness opportunities through placements and multicultural education classes should provide them with a more comprehensive understanding of serving children in our nation's schools (Dee, 2012).

Therefore, it is the responsibility of teacher preparation programs to provide candidates with the knowledge, skills, and disposition to understand and value differences among cultures and ethnicities. Within the curriculum, courses that provide educators opportunities to gain additional understanding and appreciation for diversity should be designed. It should be stressed to educators that respect for diversity encompasses much more than an understanding of a child's ethnicity.

In summary, first-year early childhood education demands that educators be well versed in numerous facets, including teaching young children, research grounded in early childhood, cultural competence, and continued professional development. Further qualification may assure that these successful outcomes are met. Culturally responsive professional leadership development is necessary for the advancement of PKEs and therefore remains paramount for the improvement of education in the nation.

ATE STANDARDS

The Association of Teacher Education Standards (ATE, n.d.) are vetted by teacher educators in the profession, and the goals therein support educators at all phases of their career, to include early childhood teachers. Therefore, the purpose of this mixed-methods case study was to examine the impact of ATE Standards to 38 PKEs in several rural sites in state and/or federally funded preschool programs in southeastern classrooms.

DEFINITION OF SELECTED TERMS

For purposes of this study, specific terms have been selected as key definitions toward supporting the reader's understanding of terminology and implementation throughout the discussion. *Site* is defined as the dwelling in which the classroom resides. *Classroom* is defined as the state-funded learning environment whereby children and educators work together on a daily basis.

Pre-kindergarten is operationally defined as a program designed to provide a classroom-based learning environment through high standards and instruction for 4-year-old children. *State-funded classroom* is operationally defined as a classroom that receives funding for operation from the state in which the pre-kindergarten classroom resides. The funding is used for the operational budget which is inclusive of items such as teacher salaries, instructional supplies and materials, and professional development.

METHOD

Nineteen pre-kindergarten classrooms housed in 15 different sites located in the southeastern part of the Unites States were selected via purposeful sampling. Each pre-kindergarten classroom has one lead teacher and one assistant teacher assigned. The pre-kindergarten classrooms are part of the state funded pre-kindergarten program.

Thirty-eight pre-kindergarten (PK) educators who serve in the role of lead or assistant pre-kindergarten teacher in a state-funded program located in the southeastern part of the United States were identified for the study. Of the 38 educators, 18 were identified as being first-year (less than an academic school year in their assigned role) educators. In these 19 pre-kindergarten classrooms, six educators were purposively selected from the sample pool of participants to answer a structured interview protocol.

First, the researchers collected quantitative data available in datasets related to demographics, educational attainment, and number of years of experience of the educator, to analyze descriptive, correlation, and regression analyses of these selected variables. Next, the researchers conducted observations on the classroom environment, classroom, and management.

During these observational visits, educators stated various apprehensions and asked questions for clarity and assistance as they sought to understand the expectations of the research participant and the state-funded program. The researchers were higher education professors and former pre-K educators and took the teachers concerns into consideration in the observations.

One of the researchers served as an observer in classroom settings. This researcher recorded field notes from observations in the classroom settings. These field notes were used to construct post-conference interview questions with classroom educators. In order to assure the validly and credibility of the study two researchers analyzed the transcripts and a third researcher provided a member check. The ATE Standards guided the qualitative analysis of the data.

Triangulation of the data analysis was sought by reviewing the notes gathered by the researcher who had prima facie access to observing the subjects in their natural setting; the collection of demographic variables used to quantify the participants' experiences as pre-K teachers and the currency of the findings compared to the ATE Standards were identified to ascertain an analysis. This research process was designed to support the effort to capture not only quantitative data but also the perceived lived classroom experiences of the educators that could be transcribed for analyses of the classroom experiences shared by the participants.

FINDINGS AND DISCUSSION

The total numbers of educators (N = 38) for the sample available for analyses from the data collection procedure were those employed in the state-funded pre-kindergarten classrooms. Eighteen educators (47%; n = 18) were identified as first-year educators teaching in the state-funded pre-kindergarten classroom. Twenty (53%; n = 20) educators were identified as returning educators to the state-funded pre-kindergarten classroom.

New Pre-kindergarten Educators vs. Returning Pre-kindergarten Educators

Educators identify as black; one lead teacher identifies as Hispanic (2.6%; n = 1) and one (2.6%; n = 1) lead teacher identifies as Native American. Conversely, 13 (34%; n = 13) of the assistant educators identify as black; five (13%; n = 5) of the assistant teachers identify as white and one (2.6%; n = 1) assistant teacher identifies as Hispanic.

Facility Type

Eleven (58%; n = 11) are defined as public school classrooms. Three (16%; n = 3) are defined as privately owned childcare center classrooms. Five (26%; n = 5) are defined as Head Start classrooms. The researchers, as cited from the procedures identified, selected variables related to degree attainment, first-year teaching at pre-K level within the state agency (yes or no), number of years of teaching experience, number of years in pre-K teaching experience regardless of location and the coding of the ethnic group for which the pre-K teacher identified.

It is understood that the demographic variable of ethnicity was not used as an indicator for the analysis related to the research; however, the researchers coded the ethnicity for descriptive statistical analyses for educational attainment that may pertain to another research focus.

Statistical Analyses From Pre-K Program

Table 4.1 provides the mean and standard deviation for the variables: highest educational degree attained (m = 2.54; SD = .900); first-year teaching in state pre-K (less than an academic school year; m= 1.47; SD = .506); number of years of teaching experience (m = 5.79; SD = 6.222), and number of years of pre-K experience (m = 2.68; SD = 3.8884).

The researchers (one of whom observed the settings over a period of time) perceived that pre-K teaching experience is the variable that may be significant in the overall effectiveness of educators responsible for children in the pre-K classroom settings. However, correlation is not causation, so the statistical analysis can only provide a glimpse into one case study from a group of educators operating in a larger statewide service area.

Therefore, Pearson Correlation Coefficient was used to verify the relationship between number of years of pre-K experience and selected variables of education and experiences teaching collected about classroom educators. The theory of the variables suggests that the population of students served and the potential need for understanding the learner should be measured against related variables of teaching experience. Hence, Pearson Product Moment

Table 4.1. Mean and Standard Deviation for the Variables

Variable	Mean	Standard Deviation	Number
Ethnic Group	1.61	0.679	38
Highest Educational Degree Attained	2.54	0.900	37
First-Year Teaching in State Pre-K*	1.47	0.506	38
Number of Years of Teaching Experience	5.79	6.222	38
Number of Years of Pre-K Experience	2.68	3.884	38

* Less than an academic school year.

Correlation suggests that a relationship can be positive or negative from a review of the computation found from the statistical procedure (Kalla, 2011). For this research analyses focused of the relationships between the "Number of Years of Pre-Experience" as the Dependent Variable (DV) with other collected variables.

Therefore, Table 4 provided the results of the Pearson r correlation of the selected variables to determine the relationship between "Number of Years of Pre-K Experience" and the independent variables (N = 38). "First Year Teaching in Pre-K" (yes or no) had a negative correlation (r = −.623 with a two tailed significance of .000), and " Number of Years of Teaching Experience" resulted in a positive correlation coefficient (r = .694 with a two-tailed significance of .000). The researchers acknowledge that correlation is not causation, but are reporting the relationship between the collected variables from the specific population as cited in Table 4.

Separately, As reflected from Table 4.2, there was a negative statistically significant relationship between the independent variables "Number of years of Teaching Experience" and "Number of Years Teaching in PreK" (r = −.422 with significance of .008; N = 38).

Table 4.3 provided Model Summary results for the variables that were predictors for the constant PK teaching experience. As reflected, these variables were "Number of Years of Teaching Experience" and First-Year Teaching in PK." The model 1 output resulted in r = .689; r2 = .475; standard error of 2.875; F change = 31.617; df1 = 1; df2 = 35 sig. of .000). Model 2 resulted in r2 of .610; standard error of 2.513; F change = 11.831; df1 = 1; df2 = 34 and sig. of .002).

The next output, cited on Table 4.4, was the Coefficients Among the Variables. The output included the amount of collinearity from the regression (Hair, Anderson, Tatham, & Black, 1995). The Coefficients Among the Variables, Table 4.4, provided the unstandardized betas, standardized betas' t-values, significance, and collinearity statistics. Model 1 of the analysis reflected the output for years of teaching experience reported as follows: The beta coefficient was .432 unstandardized; standard error of .077 with a standardized Beta of .689; t value = 5.623; and significance of .000. Model 1 collinearity Statistics resulted in a tolerance = 1.00 and the VIF = 1.00.

Model 2 cited from Table 4.4 from the Coefficients Among the Variables analysis provided the following results: unstandardized beta .330; standard

Table 4.2. Correlations

Variable		Ethnic Group	Gender	Highest Educational Degree Attained	First-Year Teaching in State Pre-K*	Number of Years of Teaching Experience	Number of Years of Pre-K Experience
Ethnic Group	Pearson Correlation	1	.148	.071	-.228	.248	.095
	Sig. (two-tailed)		.374	.676	.169	.133	.571
	N	38	38	37	38	38	38
Gender	Pearson Correlation	.148	1	-.086	-.173	-.193	.115
	Sig. (2-tailed)	.374		.612	.298	.245	.491
	N	38	38	37	38	38	38
Highest Educational Degree Attained	Pearson Correlation	.071	-.086	1	-.195	.179	.165
	Sig. (2-tailed)	.676	.612		.248	.290	.330
	N	37	37	37	37	37	37
First-Year Teaching in State Pre-K (less than an academic school year)	Pearson Correlation	-.228	-.173	-.195	1	-.422**	-.623**
	Sig. (2-tailed)	.169	.298	.248		.008	.000
	N	38	38	37	38	38	38
Number of Years of Teaching Experience	Pearson Correlation	.248	-.193	.179	-.422**	1	.694**
	Sig. (2-tailed)	.133	.245	.290	.008		.000
	N	38	38	37	38	38	38
Number of Years of Pre-K Experience	Pearson Correlation	.095	.115	.165	-.623**	.694**	1
	Sig. (2-tailed)	.571	.491	.330	.000	.000	
	N	38	38	37	38	38	38

* Less than an academic school year.
** Correlation is significant at the 0.01 level (two-tailed).

Table 4.3. Model Summary

Model	R	R Square	Adjusted R Square	Std. Error of the Estimate	Change Statistics				
					R Square Change	F Change	df1	df2	Sig. F Change
1	.689[a]	.475	.460	2.875	.475	31.617	1	35	.000
2	.781[b]	.610	.587	2.513	.136	11.831	1	34	.002

[a] Predictors: (Constant), Number of Years of Teaching Experience.
[b] Predictors: (Constant), Number of Years of Teaching Experience, First-Year Teaching in State Pre-K (less than an academic school year).

Table 4.4. Coefficients[a] Among the Variables

Model	Unstandardized Coefficients		Standardized Coefficients	t	Sig.	Collinearity Statistics	
	B	Std. Error	Beta			Tolerance	VIF
1 (Constant)	.185	.658		.282	.780		
Number of Years of Teaching Experience	.432	.077	.689	5.623	.000	1.000	1.000
2 (Constant)	5.352	1.608		3.328	.002		
Number of Years of Teaching Experience	.330	.074	.525	4.480	.000	.835	1.198
First-Year Teaching in State Pre-K (less than an academic school year)	−3.121	.907	−.403	−3.440	.002	.835	1.198

[a] Dependent Variable: Number of years of Pre-K Experience.

error of .074; the standardized beta coefficient of .525; with a t value = 4.480 and significance of .000.

Model 2 Collinearity Statistics for model 2 produced a Tolerance = .835 and VIF of 1.198. Hence, Multicollinearity Diagnostics resulted in VIF of 1.198 for the variables in the output for Table 4.4 Coefficients Among the Variables.

The results from the Model Summary (Table 4.3) and Coefficients Among the Variables (Table 4.4) provides a statistical analysis of the variables collected for the population of PreK Teachers identified related to teaching experiences, First Year Teaching in State PreK Setting with the of years of PreK experience. The two variables were statistically significant but are not suggested to be causal relationships for effectiveness in teaching of preschool children. It is suggested that the collection of teaching experiences cited for the observed PK

Teachers identified with an areas serving children resulted in relationships that provides a glimpse into current types of experiences of the teachers. The need for interviews from observations manifested from the data analyses.

REPORT FROM PRE-K TEACHER OBSERVATIONS AND INTERVIEWS

The tables that follow (Tables 4.5, 4.6, 4.7, 4.8, and 4.9) provide a glimpse on results from the researcher participant's observations of the selected

Table 4.5. Post Observation Participant Response Analyses Matrix A

Pre-K Participants	Years of Previous Teaching Experience	Summary I of Transcribed Responses	Summary II of Transcribed Responses
P1 **ATE Standard 3** Master teacher educators: Inquire systematically into, and reflect on, their own practice and demonstrate commitment to lifelong professional development.	8 years of teaching experience. P1 had previous experience teaching children Birth-Five. P1 is a first-year lead teacher and serves in the same classroom with P2.	During the post observation feedback session, P1 and P2 stated the following: I don't feel supported. You just don't know what we go through. There is a real lack of communication. Every time we try and talk to our [supervisor] [the supervisor] just passes us by.	Having more support from my immediate supervisor is what we need in order to be more successful.
P2 **ATE Standard 3** Master teacher educators: Inquire systematically into, and reflect on, their own practice and demonstrate commitment to lifelong professional development.	1 year of teaching experience with children Birth-Five. P2 is a first-year assistant teacher and serves in the same classroom with P1.	During the post observation feedback session, P1 and P2 stated the following: I don't feel supported. You just don't know what we go through. There is a real lack of communication. Every time we try and talk to our [supervisor] [the supervisor] just passes us by.	Having more support from my immediate supervisor is what we need in order to be more successful.

Table 4.6. Post Observation Participant Response Analyses Matrix B

Pre-K Participants	Previous Teaching Experience Description	Summary I of Transcribed Responses	Summary II of Transcribed Responses
P3 **ATE Standard 3** Master teacher educators: Inquire systematically into, and reflect on, their own practice and demonstrate commitment to lifelong professional development.	20 years of teaching experience. P3 is serving as a first-year pre-kindergarten lead teacher whose previous teaching experience consists of teaching 2nd grade.	I feel like I have a better understanding of what I am supposed to do now. Going to see another classroom really helped. I really just didn't know what I was supposed to do. The biggest issue we faced was that the kids didn't know how to play.	I needed to see someone else in action so that I would have a better idea of what was expected of me.

Table 4.7. Post Observation Participant Response Analyses Matrix C

Pre-K Participants	Previous Teaching Experience	Summary I of Transcribed Responses	Summary II of Transcribed Responses
P4 **ATE Standard 3** Master teacher educators: Inquire systematically into, and reflect on, their own practice and demonstrate commitment to lifelong professional development.	0 years of teaching experience. P4 is a recent college graduate with a bachelor's degree in early childhood education. P4 is a lead teacher.	The parents are always asking what do they do . . . They're like it seems like all they do is play? Well how do we show what they are doing if we can't give homework? I felt as if we were over thinking it. POST Visit—It really helped to see another classroom in action. We rearranged the room and I feel it works better now. I felt like we were over thinking it.	I am trying to find the middle ground between parents and guidelines. POST VISIT—Once I was able to see other children and teachers in a classroom setting I was able to restructure my classroom.

Table 4.8. Post Observation Participant Response Analyses Matrix D

Pre-K Participants/ ATE Standard Recommended	Previous Teaching Experience	Summary I of Transcribed Responses	Summary II of Transcribed Responses
P5 **ATE Standard 3** Master teacher educators: Inquire systematically into, and reflect on, their own practice and demonstrate commitment to lifelong professional development.	2 years of teaching experience. P5 is a first year pre-k teacher serving in the role of lead teacher. P5 was previously a 4th-grade teacher.	I'm just trying to get accustomed to pre-k. It's so different than teaching 4th grade. I just didn't understand what I was supposed to do. Now that I have a grasp on everything, it's better.	Pre-kindergarten and 4th grade are completely different. I have a better understanding of what is required.

Table 4.9. Post Observation Participant Response Analyses Matrix E

Pre-K Participants	Previous Teaching Experience	Summary I of Transcribed Responses	Summary II of Transcribed Responses
P6 **ATE Standard 3** Master teacher educators: Inquire systematically into, and reflect on, their own practice and demonstrate commitment to lifelong professional development.	0 years of teaching experience. P6 is a recent college graduate with bachelor's degree in child development.	Well, that's not how they taught us to do it in school. What are we supposed to do? How are we supposed to handle when they don't listen and we've tried redirection?	The way I was taught in school and what I am experiencing in the classroom are not the same.

educators in the pre-K classrooms. The reporting of the educators suggested that ATE Standards could promote teacher efficacy and professional growth. The results from the interviews are provided as follows (Tables 4.5, 4.6, 4.7, 4.8, and 4.9).

SUMMARY AND RECOMMENDATIONS

The Association of Teacher Education Standards have been vetted by teacher educators in the profession. The most significant period of human life is during the preschool years of human development. It is highly recommended the ATE Standards be viewed as a potential focus for professional development. The analysis suggested that the shared experiences of educators identified for this study from state-funded programs for children in the United States of America should have teacher educators poised to connect their lived experiences with a set of standards in the field.

This mixed-methods case study of a small sample size should be expanded or replicated to ascertain the level of significance for the selected variables and the use of the observations as a tool for teacher reflections on their practice, instead of a punitive process for evaluation. It appears from the small sample that the post-observation interviews using ATE Standard 3 as the overarching framework produced responses that may contribute to the development of master teacher professional growth.

It is suggested that other ATE Standards should be purposefully used to frame instructional coaching with pre-K educators, so our nation's classrooms can have master educators in every classroom where our most impressionable and vulnerable children are being served.

Since the classroom settings for this research were all rural, it has been observed by the researchers that professional development designed to advance the master teacher capacity of pre-K educators should include training in the sociology of the environment served; the understanding of students with disabilities; and collaboration with social workers. Particularly, early learning environments with effective pre-K teacher educators emerging as master teachers (ATE Standard 3) should reflect upon early detection of students with disabilities.

For example, the identification of preschoolers to special education services can occur in various ways. Children who are seen regularly for wellness check-ups by their pediatrician are referred to developmental pediatricians or other specialists if there are any questions regarding a child's development. Children can also be identified for special education services through the local Child Find office. As an IDEA (the Individuals With Disabilities Education Act) requirement, each state must have wide-ranging systems of child find offices in order to identify, locate, and evaluate children with disabilities.

It is not unusual for a daycare provider, a babysitter, or a preschool staff member to inform a parent about a possible developmental or learning delay. Of course, parents are not required to wait for someone else to express concerns about their child's development. They can contact the local Child Find office through their local school system, and arrange to have their child screened and/or evaluated.

Since preschool staff members are adults who have been identified as persons who are expected to notify parents of any developmental concerns, it is pertinent that these providers are adequately equipped with the skills to support overall child development and formal school academic readiness.

Thus, it is paramount for educators and administrators in pre-K classrooms housed within private agencies and faith-based centers to promote effective systematic professional development. Most glaringly for the future of the children it is recommended that ATE Standard 3 be conceptualized at the very basic level of human understanding by all caregivers of young children.

REFERENCES

Adler (1982). The paideia proposal: An educational manifesto. New York, NY: MacMillan Publishing Company.

Anderson, J. D. (1988). *The education of blacks in the south, 1860–1935*. Chapel Hill, NC: University of North Carolina Press.

Association of Teacher Educators. (n.d.). Standards for teacher educators. Retrieved from http://www.ate1.org/pubs/uploads/tchredstdst0308.pdf

Avalos, B. (2011). Teacher professional development in teaching and teacher education over ten years. *Teaching and Teacher Education, 27*(1), 10–20.

Barnett, W. S., Carolan, M. E., Squires, J. H., & Clarke Brown, K. (2014). The state of preschool 2013: First look. National Center for Education Statistics. Research Report NCES 2014-078. U.S. Department of Education.

Blase, J., Blase, J. (2004). *Handbook of instructional leadership*: How successful principals promote teaching and learning. Thousand Oaks, CA: Corwin Press.

Cahan, E.D. (1989). *Past caring: A history of U.S. preschool care and education for the Poor, 1820–1965*. National Center for Children in Poverty. Columbia University.

Darling-Hammond, L. (2010). The flat word and education: How America's commitment to equity will determine our future. New York, NY: Teachers College Press.

Dee, A.L. (2012). Evidence of cultural competence within teacher performance assessments. *Action in Teacher Education, 34*, 262–275.

Del Prado Hill, P., Friedland, E. S., & Phelps, S. (2012). How teacher candidates' perceptions of urban students are influenced by field experiences: A review of the literature. *Action in Teacher Education, 34*(1), 77–96.

Georgia Department of Early Care and Learning. (2015). Retrieved from http://decal.ga.gov/Pre-K/Pre-KHome.aspx

Hair, J. F., Jr., Anderson, R. E., Tatham, R. L., & Black, W. C. (1995). *Multivariate data analysis* (3rd ed). New York, NY: Macmillan.

Kalla, S. (2011, July 26). *Relationship Between Variables*. Retrieved from https://explorable.com/relationship-between-variables

Kamerman, S. B., & Gatenio-Gabel, S. (2007). Early childhood education and care in the United States: An overview of the current policy picture. *International Journal of Child Care and Education Policy, 1(1), 23–34*.

Ladson-Billings, G. (2009). *The dream-keepers: Successful teachers of African-American children*. San Francisco, CA: Jossey-Bass.

Moffett, N. L., Dove, C. A. (Eds.) (2015). Pearls of wisdom from a woman of color, courage and commitment: Pearlie Craft Dove. Bloomington, IN: Xlibris.

Northhouse, P.G. (2010). *Leadership: Theory and practice*. Thousand Oaks, CA: Sage Publications.
Remarks by the President in the State of the Union Address. (2013, August 9). Speech presented at State of the Union Address in D.C., U.S. Capitol Washington. Retrieved from https://www.whitehouse.gov/the-press-office/2013/02/12/remarks-president-state-union-address
Roosevelt, D. (2011). To see is not to own: Child study as a practice of attention for beginning teachers. *The New Educator, 7*(3), 240–273.
The Atlantic. (2013, February 12). *Obama's 2013 State of the Union Speech: Full Text*. Available from https://www.theatlantic.com/politics/archive/2013/02/obamas-2013-state-of-the-union-speech-full-text/273089/

Chapter 5

Teacher Educators as Collegial Mentors

Integrating Instructional Technologies through an Extended Community of Practice Professional Development Approach

Caroline M. Crawford

ABSTRACT

Communities of practice have been recognized as living, breathing realities since the earliest days of social engagement and connection. Within this understanding, a microcosm of connection, collegiality, and facilitative support is the pre-kindergarten thru twelfth grade realities of the U.S. education system. The symbiotic learning landscape of the teacher education efforts engages in a metaphoric dance wherein teacher educators and teacher candidates learn from one another. Within this discussion, our focus is upon the findings from teacher educators coming together in a graduate instructional technology course experience that inherently shifted teacher educator perspectives from professional, personal, and self-efficacy recognitions that grew from a community of practice online landscape and embraced social engagement, community-fluid connections, and collegial mentorship. The resulting theoretical implications suggest an evolving self-efficacy of teacher educators as collegial mentors, emphasizing thematic realities of support within learning landscapes of practice.

KEYWORDS

collegiality, collegial mentors, collegial mentorship, self-efficacy, social engagement

INTRODUCTION: FRAMING THE DISCUSSION

The landscape of the preK-12 education system has shifted over the decades, engaging in differentiated practices and professional efforts that were led and framed by teacher educators. As introduced by Etienne Wenger (1998), a conversation that began with the question, "So, what if we adopted a different perspective, one that placed learning in the context of our lived experience of participation in the world?" (p. 3; Wenger, 2009, p. 210).

This question brilliantly frames the field-based teacher education community. Engaging learning within a real-world environment supports not only the learner's cognitive engagement and social discourse understandings as framed through Wittgenstein's work (1961; Burr, 2015; Gorski, 2016; Gupta, 2016; Inwood, 2015; Shotter, 2016) but also the development of conceptual frameworks of understanding as framed by Vygotsky (1933/1966, 1935, 1981; Barwell, 2016; Esteban-Guitart, 2015; Metraux, 2015; Montealegre, 2016; Wang, 2015).

With the introduction of the Digital Age, also referred to as the Information Age, the introduction of technological support within the instructional process was also perceived as a ubiquitous shift in the learning and training processes. Perhaps the most interesting aspect associated with the Digital Age is the lack of impact that has actually occurred over the past two decades. There has been an overlay of technological implementation as an afterthought, an add-on; yet only recently has the shift toward technology as a useful and integral instructional tool begun to reach the realms of recognition.

The reality of the situation is that it has taken time for the technological tools to not only reach monetary realities that allowed for everyday people to afford the technologies currently available, but also that the technological tools have developed a welcome portability and quality of product that supports instructional efforts. Further, the Internet access and open Wi-Fi capabilities that have developed into a real-world support structure and engagement within not only the school sites but also within community-based environments have shifted the thought process significantly.

Today, anyone can purchase a coffee at the local Starbuck's and then sit for hours enjoying free Wi-Fi availability, as well as a growing number of community-based environments that free the technological user from the bounds of password-protected Wi-Fi access.

This impact has shifted instructional technology efforts and motivational considerations (Maslow, 1943, 1954, 1962, 1968, 1964/1970a, 1970b), including Vroom's expectancy theory (1964; Chen, Ellis, & Suresh, 2016; Hung, Zhuang, & Lin, 2015; Lăzăroiu, 2015; Parsons & Goff, 1978; Purvis, Zagenczyk, & McCray, 2015; Shweiki, Martin, Beekley, Jenoff, Koenig, Kaulback, Lindenbaum, Patel, Rosen, Weinstein, Zubair, & Cohen, 2015; Whittington, 2015) that are deeply embedded in the instructional experience and integration of instructional technologies.

PROBLEM

Considering the potential shifts in instructional technology that have recently occurred, I began looking at the disconnect between the technology-based teacher education coursework discussions that were occurring, how the coursework shifts and supports the field-based teacher educator efforts, and the tool-focused versus instruction-focused efforts within the courses under discussion.

I desired to shift the conversation within the teacher education technology courses, toward the instructional implementation of different technological tools that were focused upon engaging teacher educators in recognizing the possibilities revolving around technologies that could make their work easier to achieve; this recognition is focused not only upon the instructional impact but also upon the professional comfortableness, dispositions, and connection needs inherent within the field.

PURPOSE

The purpose of this study was to further the understanding of the impact of a graduate instructional technology course upon field-based classroom teachers as the shift toward a recognition and realization of their own teacher educator roles was realized. The inherent focus upon the applications of instructional technology tools within *real-world* differentiated learning landscapes and communities of practice for each learner was integrally important. The impact of the graduate course was not only realized by the enrolled classroom teachers, but the shifting understanding and professional roles extended into a recognition of each person as a teacher educator and collegial mentor.

SIGNIFICANCE

Through this reflective process, I decided that the most appropriate progression forward would be to redesign a graduate course that was focused upon teacher educators who were all teacher educators: current classroom teachers, instructional leads, and developing academic leaders. Recognizing the subject matter expertise that each professional brought to the course, it was my desire to build upon the learner's own subject matter expertise by engaging the instructional technologies within their own real-world professional realms. As such, the frame of the course developed into a community of practice acknowledgment that supported a professional development approach.

This professional development approach was not only engaged by the course learners but also focused upon an extended community impact approach, wherein the learners were mandated to share their technological products with their real-world communities of friends, family, work colleagues, work supervisors, and graduate program colleagues and professors. The extended community of practice approach directly impacted the motivational efforts as teacher educator professionals, slowly developing the self-efficacy of the learners as well as developing the collegial mentorship and leadership recognition within a metaphoric "learning in a landscape of practice" approach (Wenger-Trayner, Fenton-O'Creevy, Hutchinson, Kubiak, & Wenger-Trayner, 2015).

This understanding goes beyond the realm of singular-impact communities of practice that disburse after a designated period of time, toward the larger realm of real-world implementation and engagement that continues the potential impact within teacher educators' professional communities. This long-term potential impact shifts teacher educators from singular-impact individuals toward collegial mentors with considerations toward extended community of practice professional development approaches.

STANDARDS FOR TEACHER EDUCATORS

The Association of Teacher Educators' Standards for Teacher Educators (ATE, n.d.) reflect dispositions, indicators, and artifacts that fully represent quality teacher educator professional understandings and efforts. Within the differentiated standards, this manuscript discussion reflects upon the following nine standards: STANDARD 1 Teaching, STANDARD 2 Cultural Competence, STANDARD 3 Scholarship, STANDARD 4 Professional Development, STANDARD 5 Program Development, STANDARD 6 Collaboration, STANDARD 7 Public Advocacy, STANDARD 8 Teacher Education Profession, and STANDARD 9 Vision (ATE, n.d., pp. 1–8). This manuscript specifically reflects upon *Standard 4 Professional Development* (ATE, n.d., p. 4), as the description states the following:

STANDARD 4 Professional Development

Inquire systematically into, reflect on, and improve their own practice and demonstrate commitment to continuous professional development.

Accomplished teacher educators help pre-service and in-service teachers with professional development and reflection, and model examples from their personal development, making transparent the goals, information, and changes for improvements in their own teaching. Teacher educators examine their own beliefs and contributions of life experiences. There is a vital link established between belief and action (Vygotsky, 1978). Reflective practice of teachers can occur in several forms and at different times during and after an event, and should be proactive in nature to guide any future action (Farrell, 2004).

Reflection can affect professional growth and bring individuals to greater self-actualization (Pedro, 2006) through collaboration with others to apply knowledge and experiences into practice (Schön, 1996). Experience is key to developing thinking (Dewey, 1916) and helping educators to form knowledge, collect data, reflect on that data, and make changes to their practices. (ATE, n.d., p. 4)

Through this graduate course and associated qualitative study effort, the professional development engagement associated with teacher candidate and classroom teacher extended community of influence and impact is clearly articulated as a collaborative collegial mentorship effort. This more clearly reflects upon teacher educators as collegial mentors, by reaching beyond the bounds of a professional development experience and into a metaphoric "learning in a landscape of practice" engagement and reflective real-world approach (Wenger-Trayner et al., 2015).

FRAMING THE ENVIRONMENT

The graduate course environment engages the same catalog description as other *Application of Technology* graduate courses, designed and taught by other instructors:

Prerequisite: Basic computer literacy

Students will learn how to use interactive Internet-based software applications that facilitate the work of instructional designers, teachers, school administrators and school counselors. Students engage in projects such as developing blogs, online courses, instructional videos, podcasts, rubrics, online tests, surveys, portfolios, and organizing information. The history of instructional technology, learning theory as applied to instructional technology, and the principles of data processing are reviewed. (University of Houston-Clear Lake, n.d., para. 1)

The course objectives are differentiated from other *Applications of Technology* courses, yet the final course product must be maintained as a final electronic portfolio website. As such, the course objectives are designated toward supporting assignments that embed technology within collegial team-based deliverables, technology-based deliverables with instructionally appropriate embedding, strong reflective practitioner understandings, and an evaluation of the course embedded efforts through an analysis framed within the International Society for Technology in Education (ISTE) Standards.

Within the initial course period, the learners must address the following technological expectations: VAIL Tutor "Certificate of Successful Completion" (University of Maryland University College, 2015); set up a Zoom.com personal video conference account (Zoom Video Communications, Inc., 2016); set up a personal Dropbox or WeTransfer account (Dropbox, Inc., n.d.; WeTransfer BV, 2016); set up a YouTube Channel for the course (YouTube, LLC, 2016); and set up a website for the course.

Within each of the primary course units, there are specific assignment expectations: assignment technology implementation, team video-based critical analysis discussion, and bulletin board assignment (Part One: Team-Based; Part Two: Individual Posts, Community-Based Analyses and Unit Experience Reflections). Although the assignments are explicitly parallel toward a level of uniformity of self-regulated expectation, each of the assignments is differentiated due to assigned readings, technology implementation topics and associated tools to analyze and implement, and the bulletin board discussions.

RESEARCH QUESTIONS

As the purpose of this study was to further the understanding of the impact of a graduate instructional technology course upon field-based classroom teachers as the shift toward a recognition and realization of their own teacher educator roles was realized, the research question of inquiry was designated: How did this course impact the teacher educator's understanding of learning in a landscape of practice?

RESEARCH METHODOLOGY AND DESIGN

The nature of this qualitative study is an instrumental multiple case study approach (Stake, 2005) that implements personal documents (Bogdan & Biklen, 2007) and personal communications as the sources for descriptive data. As Stake suggests, "The case is undertaken because, first and last, one wants better understanding of this particular case" (p. 445); specifically, the multiple case study is focused upon three graduate course experiences that extend over three separate semesters. The emphasis upon a multiple case study approach is the contextual differentiations between instructional environments, being the online, and blended learning environment approaches.

As stated by Baxter and Jack (2008), "In a multiple case study, we are examining several cases to understand the similarities and differences between the cases" (p. 550). Results from a multiple case study approach "[are] considered robust and reliable" (Baxter & Jack, 2008, p. 550), suggesting the approach is appropriate toward this study focus.

The expectation focused upon an instrumental multiple case study approach (Stake, 1995) focuses upon the understanding that this approach chooses the same course experience over multiple semesters, and that includes multiple different graduate students, toward learning about the effects of the technology course experiences upon the teacher educators. The issues revolving around instructional technologies and the embedding of the instructional technologies within the teacher educator professional and instructional lives are the dominant consideration in this study.

Participants

The participants were graduate students who self-selected to enroll in a graduate *Applications of Technology* course that was designed, developed, and implemented by the course instructor. Some graduate students enrolled in the course as a core graduate course that was mandated toward completing a graduate-level candidate plan of study, and other participants enrolled in the course as one of innumerable electives from which the graduate student could choose to enroll.

The significant majority of the participants were classroom teacher educators, with a minority of participants engaging in professional career paths outside the bounds of the preK-12 educational system. The majority of participants were female, with a small minority of male participants, as it reflects the enrollment make-up of other graduate coursework throughout the college.

PROCEDURES

After obtaining internal review board approval to proceed, the researcher reviewed archived personal and unsolicited in-course communications, final course reflection manuscripts, and student course evaluation comments. All qualitative course data were accessed for analysis after the semester-based course was completed and all final grades were submitted.

DATA ANALYSIS

The data were analyzed using the grounded theory approach toward identifying patterns and themes that naturally arose through the data (Charmaz, 2014; Creswell, 2007). As clearly articulated by the term, the grounded theory approach is focused upon the development of a theoretical structure that is based, or grounded, in the data sets. As such, the data analysis within a grounded theory approach is a process, a procedural effort, within which innumerable individual participants are involved. The coding occurred by hand, implementing an open coding strategy, within a word processing environment to lay out the quotations within a table format that exponentially grew with themes and subthemes as was necessary and appropriate.

The open coding approach (Strauss & Corbin, 1990) emphasized developing a level of comfortableness with the data sets and then led to the creation of a table format that allowed for the easy chunking of data sets toward summarizing and grouping the meaning-making effort that naturally developed from and was framed through the data. Such a focused coding effort toward generating themes and categorizing the data was necessary and appropriate, delving into the nuanced communications and professional understandings of the participant pool.

A constant comparative analytical method (Glaser & Strauss, 1967) toward analysis was emphasized throughout the coding and theory building efforts associated with this approach. The nonlinear nature of the coding and analytical efforts emphasizes the connectedness and insights of the rich data sets and reflective musings and analytical efforts of the grounded theorist.

FINDINGS

Wenger's conception of learning in landscapes of practice (Wenger, 1998, 2009; Wenger-Trayner et al., 2015) is a realistic approach toward reflecting the realities in which teacher educators currently find themselves. Teacher educators have every opportunity to develop into stronger collegial mentors, not only through strong community of practice professional development approaches but also as modeled by strong instructional facilitators and collegial mentors.

The instrumental multiple case study approach within this current discussion was an evolution of understanding, as reflective practitioners learn as much from their learner colleagues as from their own depth of personal professional analysis.

As the cases were embedded within an instructional technology graduate course that emphasized an integration of instructional technologies into the teacher educator's professional lives, the differentiated understandings associated with the instructional technologies not only embraced a collegial approach toward "surviving" the course experience but also embraced the opportunity for each person to thrive as collegial mentors within a community of practice approach toward technological engagement that added a third prong to the instructional approach as emphasizing a professional development introductory impact within their professional community.

Within the structure of this study effort, the focus areas of student experience and course design were directly relevant to the grounded theory approach and constant comparative analytical method. Within these areas of focus, five major themes arose: self-efficacy, collegiality, creativity, knowledge base, and professional impact.

Self-Efficacy

Self-efficacy has been defined by Bandura (1986, 1991a, 1991b; Schunk, 1989) as a person's belief in his or her own ability to succeed. Within this course experience, teacher educators developed and enhanced their self-efficacy revolving around instructional technology, online course experiences, and the fears associated with implementing technology as professional communicative tools. As pulled from unsolicited participant communications:

- Student Thirteen Summer 2015: "I feel like I learned so much in this class. I was really dreading it because I was worried the technology would kill me. This is why I waited to take this as my last graduate class. I wish I would have taken this at the beginning because it was so helpful! I have so much to take back and share with my school."
- Student Twenty-Four, Summer 2015: "This course has given me the opportunity to explore them, and I have gained confidence in my ability to use them and teach my students as well. I am anxious to share my knowledge with my coworkers and future students!"
- Student Four, Summer 2016: "Again, I'm really amazed at everything we learned in such a short amount of time. This course helped change my perspective on technology. I had negative feelings and anxiety towards technology before this class. . . . This course made me realize how skewed my perception was. I now feel a lot more comfortable using these digital tools, and I know that I have not fallen behind. I now know that if I want to create something, I can! I don't need fancy skills; I just need to know what digital resources to use. Also, I have realized that I can depend more on these tools without becoming one of those people that is always on their phone. These digital tools can help make me more efficient as well as facilitate my collaboration with others. I very often work in teams, which is something that I have struggled with in the past. I now have a better understanding of how digital tools assist in making team processes more effective."
- Student Ten, Summer 2016: "Not only that, but the knowledge I have gained is unbelievable. My friends and colleagues have been impressed with what I now know and actually feel comfortable discussing and using. That would have never happened before."
- Student Ten, Summer 2016: "I started this class with nothing but fear for the unknown. After being successful the first couple of assignments

I started to crave more. Who would have thought?? Me?? Crave learning about Technology?? It is no different than a child. When they are empowered with knowledge and value they want more and perform better. I felt like a kid. I would actually get excited thinking about the next 'product' we had to produce and how I could use it in my area of specialty. In reality, my weakness was really my strength."
- Student Fifteen, Summer 2016: "Overall, this course has made me view education in a different way. I no longer resent technology as another thing I have to do because someone told me to. I see its relevance, and I see the ways in which technology, if used correctly, can really help teachers differentiate and create new mediums of teaching. I also see the need to stay up to date on technological trends."
- Student Sixteen, Summer 2016: "I feel so much more comfortable with technology after taking this course. . . . This course left me with a deeper understanding of how I can create technology to increase engagement and understanding and how to use it as a launch pad to connect with my colleagues."

Fear of the unknown, fear of the technology, anxiety and inherent intimidation by the unknown, and other aspects of unease were addressed and slowly dissipated due to the strength of the course design but more importantly the inherent course emphasis and understanding upon collegiality and the professionally supportive nature of collegial mentors throughout the course experience. This was initially modeled and emphasized by the course facilitator but was quickly reflected by the course participants.

Collegiality

An inherent relationship between professional colleagues, as based upon trust, ethical behaviors, and honorable expectations, evolves into a relationship stated as being collegial in nature. There is a common purpose, with a desired end in mind and which normally is framed through the desire to work together toward a successful experience and conclusion. As representative unsolicited participant communications:

- Student Eight, Summer 2015: "I also had the most amazing team members and learned that collaboration can truly be amazing when everyone does their part. Generally, I end up pulling the weight of my team and this is the first time we all did our part."
- Student Ten, Summer 2015: "As far as changes made to enhance the course, I was going to recommend letting us chose our own group members for the team assignments. However, creating the opportunity to work with

someone outside of our comfort zone allowed for us to grow collegiately and professionally and I would now not recommend that change. I had a great partner and we worked really well together. It made the team assignments something I looked forward to."
- Student Sixteen, Summer 2015: "I have truly loved this class this summer because I had to collaborate with my peers in a way that I had not in other online classes. Collaborative learning goes beyond answering questions and responding to other questions on a discussion board, but unfortunately, that is where many online classes end. Discussing the readings with my team via video conferencing was much more educational, in my opinion. This also allowed me to have a relationship with my team members and a sense of comradery with us helping each other out."
- Student Eighteen, Summer 2016: "In addition to discussions, team collaboration is another strength of this course. Having a good group member can defiantly make or break a course experience, luckily for me, M***** was an awesome partner and made the assignments fun and easy."
- Student Thirteen, Summer 2016: "After my group began our first video on Zoom, and my colleagues had some questions too, we helped each other get organized and understand the flow for the course. My fellow colleagues and I collaborated successfully in every aspect."
- Student Twenty-Four, Summer 2015: "I especially appreciated the many chances for collaboration with colleagues in and out of the course. It was helpful to post things to my blog or discussion and receive feedback from my peers so that I could learn and improve."
- Student Twenty, Summer 2016: "Another strength was the required Video Discussion for each unit. In my previous experience with online courses, I did not feel as *connected* with the material or my classmates. However, in this course, having that face-to-face interaction with my colleagues via Zoom multiple times a week truly made me feel connected with the material that we were learning for that unit. It also allowed for intellectual discussions and the introduction of new ideas and opinions that I really enjoyed hearing."
- Student Nineteen, Summer 2016: "The team Zoom conferences allowed us to reflect and analyze what we read through the lens of our experience, which deepened the collaborative learning."
- Student Twenty-Two, Summer 2016: "It also forces us as colleagues and teammates to work together. Often times in courses we go in with a one track mind, to finish the course get our grade and move on to the next. Dr. ******** made it so that we had to communicate in order to be successful. When I think about it that will be a vital part of becoming and maintaining a position as an administrator communicating and elaborating with others. So because of those aspects I feel that what we experience in this course is helping us to become better educators."

Within the bounds of this course experience, the participants emphasized collegiality. This collegial expectation was initially due to the emphasis placed upon collegiality by the course facilitator, through modeling as well as referring to the participants as "colleagues," and quickly reflected by the course participants as necessary levels of professional expectation within the course.

Creativity

Within the realm of instructional technology, so many of us find ourselves in an anxiety-riddled sense of self. Yet once the comfortableness of play, engagement, and enjoyment are recognized as desirable within a safe community of expectations, a sense of creativity may arise. The ability to imagine, to implement one's own subject matter expertise toward creating new and innovative ideas and project deliverables, and even to invent new ideas, are all creative endeavors. Within a teacher educator's daily professional practice, especially as collegial mentors, a recognition and respect toward creativity is an absolute. As representative unsolicited participant communications:

- Summer 2015: Course Evaluation Comment: "She inspires us to be our best while being creative."
- Student Ten, Summer 2015: "My educational experiences in the technology applications have been self-taught and I did not personally take the time to learn how to create a blog, design a web site, video conference, create digital periodicals . . . all of these were so exciting to learn how to do! Since they were built into the course and we had our own freedom to use the application that best fit our capabilities, it allowed for a deeper appreciation in learning and growing academically."
- Student Sixteen, Summer 2015: "A huge takeaway from this class for me this year is becoming more creative in ways that students are sharing class information. Why not allow them to create a website, blog, digital image publishing, video presentation or use social media to communicate their final product? In our world of technology, it seems wrong to not encourage our students to learn how to use it educationally."
- Student Fourteen, Summer 2015: "I have learned that the uses of technology are only bound by the limits of our imaginations."
- Student Three, Summer 2016: "I believe that true learning takes place when the learner is fully engaged and motivated to go beyond the parameters established by an assignment. Thus, I have to say that this course has been a great learning experience for me, in which I have explored and further developed my creativity, and which has helped me anchor into my teaching philosophy the importance of media literacy and technology usage."

- Student Twenty-One, Summer 2016: "Some of the strengths I found in this course were the opportunities to take risks. The exposure to the different resources and having to 'play' with them really helped to push my comfort zone."
- Student Three, Summer 2016: "Personally, I have come to the understanding that all these tools serve us not only to develop and improve classroom materials but to expose our students to these same tools as well. The goal is to develop students' technological proficiency, creativity, innovation, and critical thinking within interactive environments. Just like we put so much emphasis in allowing students to interact with the content, what better way to allow them to do this if it is not through their interaction with technology as well."
- Student Ten, Summer 2016: "I would almost venture to say that all teachers should be required to take a class like this one! Can you imagine how much knowledge and creativity would go flying through classrooms??"

Developing a culture in which creativity is embraced not only develops a strong community of practice environment that engages in collegial professional development approaches toward teacher educators as collegial mentors but the recognition that we all have talents and capabilities is inherent within cultures that breed learning within landscapes of professional practice.

Knowledge Base

Teacher educators show up in each professional development opportunity with a vast mass of knowledge already inherent within their professional selves. A recognition of this knowledge base is a philosophical imperative toward not only a collegial respect but also an effort toward expanding one's conceptual framework of understanding, especially toward the inclusion of instructional technologies within the powerful subject matter areas of expertise. As representative unsolicited participant communications:

- Student One, Summer 2015: "I didn't know what to expect exactly, but I certainly didn't think that I would learn as much as I did and be able to use these tools immediately with my students and colleagues."
- Student Two, Summer 2015: "This course has been an amazing experience where I have gained abundant knowledge of how to create and learn about various ways to implement technology in my teaching instructions and my own personal learning experience."
- Student Eight, Summer 2015: "I'm walking away with a ton of online resources and fresh ideas for integrating technology into my classroom this year."

- Student Twelve, Summer 2015: "As with most technology classes, it provided me with tangible skills that I could use in the immediate future."
- Student Twenty, Summer 2015: "This course has offered a lot to my work in the classroom, but it has also given me more support with my continue education through my Masters."
- Student Fourteen, Summer 2015: "For me, it forced me to work with technology in a way that I had never done before. I have gained new skills in how to create technology products like a website, blog or a podcast."
- Student Seven, Summer 2016: "I really am amazed at how much I have learned in just a month from this course. I can't wait to start trying it all out when school starts back up in August."
- Student Nineteen, Summer 2016: "I was just struck by how much this class has advanced our understanding of technology integration and what a resource you will be on your campus. Lead it, girl!"

The emphasis upon implementing the participants' new knowledge within their teacher educator and collegial mentoring roles is an impressive statement by each of the participants, as the vast majority of participants enrolled in this course experience with fears and negative prior experiences with technology, a prior technology course experience, or both.

Professional Impact

A part of the strengths within a well-designed professional development experience is the ability to swiftly shift the new knowledge and products into a real-world environment. Within this course experience, the emphasis upon the participant's specific subject matter expertise and instructional design understandings swiftly delved into deliverable products that were immediately available to implement within the teacher educator's classroom instructional environments. As well, due to the mandate for each technological product to be analyzed by professional colleagues extended the impact of the course into a more significant realm of impact. As representative unsolicited participant communications:

- Student Seven, Summer 2015: "I took away a full virtual tool box for my own graduate studies and classroom use that includes items such as my Wix Website, bookmarked research engines and the use of zoom video conferencing."
- Student Thirteen, Spring 2016: "My take aways are a mile long though I am now fully confident in web design, video conferencing, photo enhancing, surveying, blogging, podcasting, creating you tube account, reading reports

(Horizon), and research sites. These were my take aways that I can implement in both my professional career and personal use of technology."
- Student Five, Summer 2016: "Overall, I have learned so much from this course and I am glad I chose to take this course. Although I was apprehensive at the beginning, online courses are not bad at all. This experience was great for me. Not only did I gain a new friend, I gained so much knowledge about technology from readings and peers that I will use in my classroom."
- Student Eighteen, Summer 2016 "From this course I take away a greater understanding of developments in technology and how as professionals we should be utilizing them to our advantage, and not be afraid of them. It's great to not only read about new technologies but to also implement them myself."
- Student Twelve, Summer 2015: "Another strength of the course was the assignments were aligned to real world uses. I plan on using many of the assignments in my classroom."
- Student Sixteen, Summer 2015: "As I already mentioned, the key strengths of this class are the realistic ways in which you can implement the information from the course immediately in the classroom."
- Student Sixteen, Summer 2015: "This course overall was a great one because of the practical use that it shows not only in where education is going in the future, but technologies that are already in use today. Having my professional website set up is truly exciting to me because I can edit it to use this year in my classroom. I also plan to work with my team to create a website specifically designed for our program especially since Wix Sites is so user friendly to create."
- Student Sixteen, Summer 2015: "This class was very informative and, as I mentioned in my final reflection, I look forward to implementing many of the aspects that we practiced."
- Student Eleven, Summer 2016: "I think a course like this for all educators, would be really beneficial! You just learn so much, that you never knew. It really does make life so much easier."
- Student Nine, Summer 2016: "I think one of the biggest things I'll take away from this unit, and the class as a whole, is that we as contributors to the field of education cannot adopt a 'wait and see' attitude about educational technology if we want our education system to be competitive."
- Student Seven, Summer 2016: "I think it has created a spark in me that now wants to seek out the information for myself and be more of a leader in that arena. I think it has built my confidence to being able to stay in the forefront of technology, and as a librarian that will be important."
- Student Four, Summer 2016: "I'm very excited that I'm already using what I've learned in this course to help me with my other classes. I'm already

teaching others about these digital tools, and they are very excited about it too. I'm also thrilled about my classmates using what they have learned to enhance their students' learning."
- Student Ten, Summer 2016: "This class was real world learning. So many other classes are completed and you never pick the book up again, or open the spiral that has your notes. I am already thinking about all of the different ways I can actually USE the new things I have learned."

The professional impact of this course experience was not only meant to be time-impacted wherein the knowledge base was enhanced. Instead, the shift in thought process and professional understanding was the more desirable goal to achieve. As teacher educators who embrace the effort toward collegial mentorship, expanding one's understanding of not only a community of practice and not only instructional technologies, but more so enhancing the appeal of lifelong learning as a professional impact is imperative toward supporting teacher educators at all levels of engagement.

THEORETICAL IMPLICATIONS

As Wenger's original Communities of Practice (1998, 2009) understanding revolutionized the thought process evolving within the teacher education realm, the metaphoric "Learning in a Landscape of Practice" approach (Wenger-Trayner et al., 2015) further delved into the practicality of professional careers that include teacher education.

The lived experiences of teacher educators, recognizing the social realm in which the profession plays out, are difficult to understand; more so, it's an even more nuanced realm in which to induct teacher candidates as novice classroom teachers who have the necessary pedagogical knowledge bases, subject matter areas of expertise, and innumerable other informational and dispositional strengths to survive the initial few years within the profession.

As classroom teachers develop a professional self-efficacy associated with their responsibilities and roles, one may suggest that a shift begins to occur. The classroom teacher's "survival mode" slowly dissipates, and replacing this uncomfortableness and anxiety-laden, fear-based daily endeavor is the recognition of a dawning professional strength of understanding and self-efficacy. Many have called this an induction phase, which is similar to an onboarding period and culture shock phase as recognized by many within business and industry.

Yet, the classroom teacher role is not only a scientific understanding; it is also an artistic endeavor. One may metaphorically refer to teaching as a dance, a give and take between the instructional facilitator and learner participant. Or perhaps another movement metaphor is a professional chef who is cooking up an excellent five-course meal to be savored over an extended period of time, or perhaps even a toolbox metaphor that holds innumerable professional tools, tips, and tricks?

As the novice classroom teacher begins to develop an understanding of the rhythm and movement of the teaching and learning process, a professional shift begins to take place. No longer is this a novice classroom teacher. As a butterfly emerges from a tight cocoon, the novice teacher recognizes the professional nuances and understandings that allow for the spreading of the teacher's wings and to consider more creative understandings that may professionally impact the career path currently traveled.

Herein begins the introduction of the teacher educator, with the developing understanding of a community of practice that opens into a learning landscape of practice with many hills, valleys, and even mountain paths to tread. Professional development opportunities are a realistic effort, and consideration toward graduate academic achievements may be recognized as realities worthy of discovery. The winding road of the teacher educator meanders toward a sense of self-efficacy and dispositional strength, introducing a collegial mentor into one's understanding. Yet how might this occur?

Within this instrumental multiple case study approach, the focus was towards understanding the instructional technology graduate coursework impact. The ability to extend the graduate course's community reach beyond the bounds of the ivory tower and into the real-world efforts of professional PreK-12 teacher educators was realized.

The course participants developed into teacher educators as collegial mentors, extending the course outreach into professional communities of practice to impact not only the self-efficacy of the course participant but also toward opening the discussions that evolve into instructional technology microlearning events, professional development approaches within professional communities of practice, or perhaps even accolades that resulted in new positions of influence and effort within the organizational structure.

The findings suggest that the overarching themes of self-efficacy, collegiality, creativity, knowledge base, and professional impact are integrally important toward the successful growth of teacher educators as collegial mentors.

Yet consideration toward a recognition of self-efficacy shifts in instructional technology understandings may be directly influenced and impacted by the community environment in which the teacher educator finds one's self, wherein the creativity, collegiality, opportunity toward professional impact and direct enhancement of knowledge base within conceptual frameworks of understanding must be supported. This evolving self-efficacy notes the

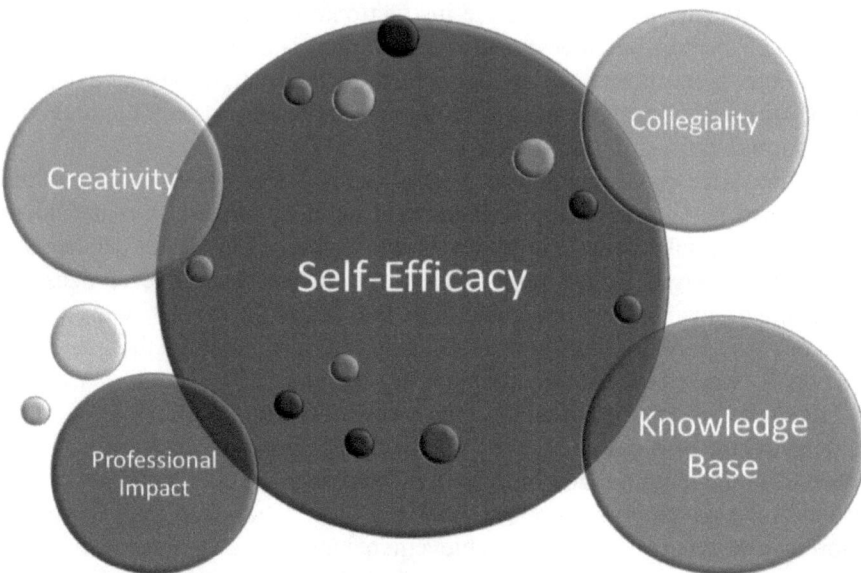

Figure 5.1. Evolving Self-Efficacy of Teacher Educators as Collegial Mentors: Thematic Realities of Support Within Learning Landscapes of Practice.

strength of impact directly supported and enhanced by the four areas of participant acknowledgment, as reflected within Figure 5.1.

LIMITATIONS

There are limitations associated with this study. First is the difficulty associated with establishing reliability and validity associated with the findings. The differentiation in foundational assumptions may reflect philosophical beliefs that are unusual or separate from another researcher's understanding of the data and subsequent analysis. As well, there is the potential for researcher bias within a study, although efforts have been made to reduce researcher bias as regards the participant pool by the introduction of aliases, method of instructional environment, or other potential biases that may occur.

Further, the interpretation of such complex social phenomena (Charmaz, 2003) as represented in this study and the subsequent theoretical frame of understanding may be interpreted in a different manner by another researcher. As well, due to the qualitative nature of the study, the findings may be difficult to parlay into useable knowledge by teacher educators beyond the scope of this study. The practical relevance of the findings may not extend beyond the specific case study.

CONCLUSIONS

Communities of practice (Wenger, 1998, 2009) were originally recognized as an extension of, although bound within, the enhanced community of learning framework. Resulting from further reflection and recognition of the nuanced understandings that a community extends beyond the bounds of an enclosed environmental arrangement, learning landscapes of practice was realized (Wenger-Trayner et al., 2015).

This approach toward understanding a shifting recognition of teacher educators as collegial mentors was studied within the bounds of a graduate instructional technology course that emphasized an extended community of practice professional development approach. This graduate course framework embraced the concept of self-efficacy as a strategic goal within the course, while supporting the development of a learner's knowledge base and associated conceptual framework of understanding, professional collegiality, a safe environment in which to support individual creativity and innovation, as well as the aforementioned extended professional impact beyond the ivory tower walls and into the real-world emphasis upon diffusion of innovations (Rogers, 1995) within the professional work place.

REFERENCES

Association of Teacher Educators (ATE). (n.d.). *Standards for Teacher Educators*. Retrieved from http://www.ate1.org/pubs/uploads/tchredstds0308.pdf

Bandura, A. (1986). *Social foundations of thought and action: A social cognitive theory*. Englewood Cliffs, NJ: Prentice-Hall.

Bandura, A. (1991a). Self-efficacy mechanism in physiological activation and health-promoting behavior. In J. Madden, IV (Ed.), *Neurobiology of learning, emotion and affect* (pp. 229–270). New York, NY: Raven.

Bandura, A. (1991b). Self-regulation of motivation through anticipatory and self-regulatory mechanisms. In R. A. Dienstbier (Ed.), *Perspectives on motivation: Nebraska symposium on motivation* (Vol. 38, pp. 69–164). Lincoln, NE: University of Nebraska Press.

Barwell, R. (2016, July). Formal and informal mathematical discourses: Bakhtin and Vygotsky, dialogue and dialectic. *Educational Studies in Mathematics 92*(3), 331–345.

Baxter, P., & Jack, S. (2008, December). Qualitative case study methodology: Study design and implementation for novice researchers. *The Qualitative Report, 13*(4), pp. 544–559. Retrieved from http://www.nova.edu/ssss/QR/QR13-4/baxter.pdf

Bogdan, R. C., & Biklen, S. K. (2007). *Qualitative research for education: An introduction to theories and methods*. Boston, MA: Allyn & Bacon.

Burr, V. (2015). *Social constructionism*. Oxfordshire, United Kingdom: Routledge.

Charmaz, K. (2003). Grounded theory—objectivist and constructivist methods. In N. K. Denzin & Y. S. Lincoln (Eds.), *Strategies of qualitative inquiry* (pp. 249–291). London: Sage.

Charmaz, K. (2014). *Constructing grounded theory*. Thousand Oaks, CA: SAGE Publications Ltd.

Chen, L., Ellis, S. C., & Suresh, N. (2016). A supplier development adoption framework using expectancy theory. *International Journal of Operations & Production Management, 36*(5), 592–615.

Creswell, J. W. (2007). *Qualitative inquiry and research design: Choosing among five traditions* (2nd ed.). Thousand Oaks, CA: Sage Publications.

Dewey, J. (1916). *Democracy and education*. New York: Macmillan.

Dropbox, Inc. (n.d.). *Dropbox*. Retrieved from https://www.dropbox.com/

Esteban-Guitart, M. (2015). LS Vygotsky and education by Moll, LC: (2014). New York, NY: Routledge, 173 pp. *Journal of Language, Identity & Education, 14*(4), 295–297.

Farrell, T.S.C. (2004). *Reflective practice in action: 80 reflection breaks for busy teachers*. Thousand Oaks, CA: Corwin Press.

Glaser, B. G., & Strauss, A. L. (1967). *The discovery of grounded theory: Strategies for qualitative research*. New York, NY: Aldine De Gruyter.

Gorski, P. S. (2016). The matter of emergence: Material artifacts and social structure. *Qualitative Sociology, 39*(2), 211–215.

Gupta, A. B. (2016). M. Foucault on knowledge and some parallels with Wittgenstein: A comparison. *Global Journal for Research Analysis, 5*(3), 108–109. Retrieved from http://worldwidejournals.in/ojs/index.php/gjra/article/viewFile/528/527

Hung, C. C., Zhuang, W. L., & Lin, C. H. (2015). The relationships among buyers' perceived risk, exhibitors' brand equity, purchase postponement and switching intention—From the perspectives of perceived risk theory and expectancy theory. *Information Management and Business Review, 7*(4), 74.

Inwood, M. (2015). Wittgenstein and Heidegger. *The Philosophical Quarterly, 66*(265): 867–869. doi: 10.1093/pq/pqv113

Lăzăroiu, G. (2015). Work motivation and organizational behavior. *Contemporary Readings in Law and Social Justice, 2*, 66–75.

Maslow, A. H. (1943). A theory of human motivation. *Psychological Review, 50*(4), 370–96.

Maslow, A. H. (1954). *Motivation and personality*. New York, NY: Harper and Row.

Maslow, A. H. (1962). *Towards a psychology of being*. Princeton, NJ: D. Van Nostrand Company.

Maslow, A. H. (1968). *Toward a psychology of being*. New York, NY: D. Van Nostrand Company.

Maslow, A. H. (1964/1970a). *Religions, values, and peak experiences*. New York, NY: Penguin.

Maslow, A. H. (1970b). *Motivation and personality*. New York, NY: Harper & Row.

Métraux, A. (2015). Lev Vygotsky as seen by someone who acted as a go-between between eastern and western Europe. *History of the Human Sciences, 28*(2), 154–172.

Montealegre, R. (2016). Controversies Piaget-Vygotsky en psicología del desarrollo/ Piaget-Vygotsky controversies in developmental psychology. *Acta Colombiana de Psicología, 19*(1).

Parsons, J. E., & Goff, S. B. (1978). Achievement & motivation: Dual modalities. *Journal of Educational Psychology, 13*, 93–96.

Pedro, J. (2006). Taking reflection into the real world of teaching. *Kappa Delta Pi Record, 42*(3), 129–133.

Purvis, R. L., Zagenczyk, T. J., & McCray, G. E. (2015). What's in it for me? Using expectancy theory and climate to explain stakeholder participation, its direction and intensity. *International Journal of Project Management, 33*(1), 3–14.

Rogers, E. M. (1995). *Diffusion of innovations* (4th ed.). New York, NY: The Free Press.

Schön, D.A. (1996). *Educating the reflective practitioner: Toward a new design for teaching and learning in the professions.* San Francisco, CA: Jossey-Bass.

Schunk, D. H. (1989). Self-efficacy and cognitive skill learning. In C. Ames & R. Ames (Eds.), *Research on motivation in education.* Vol. 3: Goals and cognitions (pp. 13–44). San Diego, CA: Academic Press.

Shotter, J. (2016). Undisciplining social science: Wittgenstein and the art of creating situated practices of social inquiry. *Journal for the Theory of Social Behaviour. 46* (1), 60–83.

Shweiki, E., Martin, N. D., Beekley, A. C., Jenoff, J. S., Koenig, G. J., Kaulback, K. R., Lindenbaum, G. A., Patel, P. H., Rosen, M. M., Weinstein, M. S., & Zubair, M. H. (2015, April 29). Applying Expectancy Theory to residency training: Proposing opportunities to understand resident motivation and enhance residency training. *Advances in Medical Education and Practice, 6*, 339–346. doi: 10.2147/AMEP.S76587

Stake, R. E. (1995). *The art of case study research.* Thousand Oaks, CA: Sage.

Stake, R. E. (2005). Qualitative case studies. In N. K. Denzin & Y. S. Lincoln (Eds.), *The Sage handbook of qualitative research* (3rd ed., pp. 443–466). Thousand Oaks, CA: Sage.

Strauss, A., & Corbin, J. (1990). *Basics of qualitative research: Grounded theory procedures and techniques.* Newbury Park, CA: Sage Publications.

University of Houston-Clear Lake. (n.d.). *INST 6031 Applications of Technology.* Retrieved from http://uhcl.smartcatalogiq.com/en/2016-2017/Graduate-Catalog/School-of-Education/INST-Instructional-Technology/6000/INST-6031

University of Maryland University College. (2015). *Academic Integrity Tutorial and Quiz.* Retrieved from http://www.umuc.edu/students/academic-integrity/ai-tutorial/academic-integrity-tutorial.html

Vroom, V. H. (1964). *Work and motivation.* New York, NY: Wiley.

Vygotsky, L. (1978). Mind in society: The development of higher psychological processes. Cambridge, MA: Harvard University Press.

Vygotsky, L.S. (1933/1966). Play and its role in the mental development of the child. *Soviet Psychology, 12*(6), 62–76.

Vygotsky, L. S. (1935). *Mental development of children during education.* Moscow-Leningrad: Uchpedgiz.

Vygotsky, L. S. (1981). The genesis of higher mental functions. In J. V. Wertsch (Ed.) *The concept of activity in Soviet psychology.* Armonk, NY: Sharpe.

Wang, R. (2015). LS Vygotsky and education. *British Journal of Educational Studies*, *63*(1), 112–114.

Wenger, E. (1998). *Communities of practice: Learning, meaning, and identity*. Cambridge, MA: Harvard University Press.

Wenger, E. (2009). A social theory of learning. In K. Illeris (Ed.), *Contemporary theories of learning: Learning theorists . . . in their own words*. New York, NY: Routledge.

Wenger-Trayner, E., Fenton-O'Creevy, M., Hutchinson, S., Kubiak, C., & Wenger-Trayner, B. (2015). *Learning in landscapes of practice: Boundaries, identify, and knowledgeability in practice-based learning*. New York, NY: Routledge.

WeTransfer BV. (2016). *WeTransfer*. Retrieved from https://www.wetransfer.com/

Whittington, K. D. (2015). Does motivation predict persistence and academic success? *Open Journal of Nursing*, *5*(01), 10.

Wittgenstein, L. (1961). *Tractatus logico-philosophicus* (Trans. D. F. Pars & B. F. McGuiness). New York, NY: Humanities Press.

YouTube, LLC. (2016). *YouTube*. Retrieved from https://www.youtube.com/

Zoom Video Communications, Inc. (2016). *Video Conferencing, Web Conferencing, Webinars, Screen Sharing—Zoom*. Retrieved from https://zoom.us/

Afterword
Caroline M. Crawford and Sandra L. Hardy

Through this text, the Association of Teacher Educators (ATE) and the ATE Commission on Classroom Teachers as Associated Teacher Educators have attempted to engage in a vital discussion that revolves around dynamic professional development principles. These principles are of integral importance in the preparation, development, and support of classroom teachers as associated teacher educators. The three separate yet related books of focus are designated as:

- *Redefining Teacher Preparation: Learning From Experience in Educator Development*
- *Dynamic Principles of Professional Development: Essential Elements of Effective Teacher Preparation*
- *Teacher to Teacher Mentality: Purposeful Practice in Teacher Education*

This book came into being, due to the vision of Nancy P. Gallavan, ATE president 2013–2014, who appointed this Commission and engaged Caroline M. Crawford as the Commission chairperson for a 3-year period.

Caroline articulated the Commission vision as the promotion of advocacy, equity, leadership, and professionalism for classroom teachers as associated teacher educators in all settings and supports quality education and collegial support for all learners at all levels. Further, the Commission mission was expressed as the promotion of quality teacher education through exemplary collaborations and collegial understandings that reflect the inherent importance of classroom teachers as associated teacher educators.

Based upon the vision, mission, and goals of the Commission's efforts, this text is meant as a *state of the profession* as it revolves around the dynamic principles of professional development pertaining to the concept of classroom teachers as associated teacher educators. This is an integrally important discussion to hold, and equally important to bring forward research and scholarly efforts toward more fully understanding and articulating the reciprocity that inherently occurs within the deep-seated cooperative relationships transpiring within the realms of teacher education.

This relationship emerges between teacher preparation programs, to professional educators within the school sites, to the teacher candidate who works with professional educators throughout the transformational journey into a student teacher and then into a novice classroom teacher. Yet within these cooperative relationships one is becoming more aware of and recognizes the deeply appreciated works of the classroom teacher who takes on significant additional mentorship and collegial professional development efforts as an associated teacher educator.

This text and the related books are an initial attempt to highlight the current understandings and associated scholarly efforts revolving around the dynamic principles of professional development pertaining to the important roles of classroom teachers as associated teacher educators.

As a historical context toward framing the place of this text, and the other two sister publications, within the teacher education professional realm, classroom teachers have recognized their roles as a multifaceted approach toward the profession. Classroom teachers have been reinventing themselves, to fit within the Information Age and toward taking on differentiated roles that may be dependent upon differentiated learning theories of Behaviorism, cognitivism, constructivism, and even connectivism, from *sage on the stage* to *facilitator* to *learner colleague* and beyond, dependent upon the instructional goals and instructional objectives.

A fun fact is that everyone has an opinion of the classroom teacher roles, including how classroom teachers should act, how classroom teachers should work, and even the different types of face-to-face, blended, and online learning environments in which classroom teachers currently find themselves engaged. Harrison and Killion (2007) stated that there are 10 roles for classroom teachers who are also actively engaged as teacher leaders, stated as being: "Resource Provider; Instructional Specialist; Curriculum Specialist; Classroom Supporter; Learning Facilitator; Mentor; School Leader; Data Coach; Catalyst for Change; and, Learner" (para. 3–21).

The Eton Institute also listed teacher roles that are inherently viable and useful within the 21st century: "The Controller; The Prompter; The Resource; The Assessor; The Organizer; The Participant; and, The Tutor" (para. 4–16). There are also innumerable researchers who desire to work out the beliefs, reasoning, and abilities of classroom teachers (Darling-Hammond, 2006; Kim, Kim, Lee, Spector, & DeMeester, 2013; Kleickmann et al., 2013; Nespor, 1987; Pajares, 1992; Putnam & Borko, 2000; Russell & Korthagen, 2013).

Yet after the researchers and scholars retreat to their offices with intriguing data sets and to work more closely with teacher candidates toward strengthening the candidate's understandings prior to the field-based experiences, a recognition arises. The depth of respect for classroom teachers as associated teacher educators undergirds a recognition of the integral and reciprocal relationships felt by all professional educators.

The identity, pedagogy, and self-efficacy embedded within the education profession is more fully realized throughout the teacher education profession due to the synchronous dance that occurs between pedagogy and andragogy, self-efficacy and mentorship that embraces modeling, and transformational journeys that directly impact one's shifting identity and sense of self no matter whether as a developing teacher educator or a burgeoning teacher leader.

REFERENCES

Darling-Hammond, L. (2006). *Powerful teacher education: Lessons from exemplary programs.* San Francisco, CA: John Wiley & Sons.

Eton Institute (n.d.). *The 7 Roles of a Teacher in the 21st Century.* Retrieved from http://etoninstitute.com/blog/teacher-training/the-7-roles-of-a-teacher-in-the-21st-century

Harrison, C., & Killion, J. (2007, September). Ten roles for teacher leaders. *Educational Leadership, 65*(1), pp. 74–77. Retrieved from http://tinyurl.com/6xf4tpq

Kim, C., Kim, M. K., Lee, C., Spector, J. M., & DeMeester, K. (2013). Teacher beliefs and technology integration. *Teaching and Teacher Education, 29*, 76–85. Retrieved from http://media.dropr.com/pdf/WEvqzmQRL2n2yxgXHBVTGHGG0tLjpzc1.pdf

Kleickmann, T., Richter, D., Kunter, M., Elsner, J., Besser, M., Krauss, S., & Baumert, J. (2013). Teachers' content knowledge and pedagogical content knowledge: The role of structural differences in teacher education. *Journal of Teacher Education, 64*(1), 90–106. doi: 10.1177/0022487112460398 Retrieved from http://tinyurl.com/j557qds

Nespor, J. (1987). The role of beliefs in the practice of teaching. *Journal of Curriculum Studies, 19*(4), 317–328. Retrieved from http://files.eric.ed.gov/fulltext/ED270446.pdf

Pajares, M. F. (1992). Teachers' beliefs and educational research: Cleaning up a messy construct. *Review of Educational Research, 62*(3), 307–332. Retrieved from http://media.dropr.com/pdf/9gnziXcoKpR4NEygcZferbvB3HonvxCa.pdf

Putnam, R. T., & Borko, H. (2000). What do new views of knowledge and thinking have to say about research on teacher learning? *Educational Researcher, 29*(1), 4–15. Retrieved from http://edu312spring13.pbworks.com/w/file/fetch/64649998/Borko%26Putnam.pdf

Russell, T., & Korthagen, F. (2013). *Teachers who teach teachers: Reflections on teacher education.* Oxfordshire, United Kingdom: Routledge.

About the Editors

Caroline M. Crawford is an associate professor of instructional technology at the University of Houston-Clear Lake in Houston, Texas. She earned her doctoral degree in 1998, with specialization areas in instructional technology and curriculum theory, and began her tenure at the University of Houston-Clear Lake (UHCL) the same year. She is also a contributing faculty member in the Walden University Richard W. Riley College of Education and Leadership's Higher Education and Adult Learning doctoral program.

Her main areas of interest focus upon communities of learning, including communities of practice and learning in landscapes of practice, and the appropriate and successful integration of technologies into the learning environment; the learning environment may be envisioned as face-to-face, blended, and online environments, as well as microlearning deliverables.

Sandra L. Hardy, Ph.D., is an active researcher, board member, and former special education teacher. She served as teacher-induction consultant and coordinator of the after-school tutoring programs for students at risk. Dr. Hardy taught G.E.D. courses and served as adjunct faculty in the graduate program for teachers and administrators where she taught advanced educational psychology. She serves as vice president to the board of the Science Center and is very active in animal rescue efforts.

Dr. Hardy is a long-time member of the Association of Teacher Educators, and continues to be involved with the organization's efforts to support teachers and administrators locally, statewide, nationally, and internationally at all levels and stages of their professional development continuum. Sandra's research interests include induction, learning communities of practice, and professional development involving professional development organizations, P-12, and higher education, respectively.

About the Contributors

Molly Abbott is a 1st grade teacher at Auburn Elementary. She began teaching kindergarten in 2010 in a charter school, and now at Auburn has evenly split the last 4 years between kindergarten and 1st grade. A graduate of Oakland University, Molly is proud to be teaching at Auburn Elementary. Not only is Auburn a partnership school, it is also the same elementary school she attended as a child. In her 3 years at Auburn, Molly has welcomed 10 field placement students into her classroom to learn and observe her teaching. Molly also speaks with preservice students about emergent literacy each semester.

Stacye A. Blount is assistant professor and assistant chairperson in the Department of Sociology at Fayetteville State University. Her research interests focus on mental health, race, teaching and learning in sociology, and African American debutante cotillions.

Yolanda Brownlee-Williams is an instructional coordinator for the Services for Exceptional Children Department. She earned a special education focus with an earned doctorate in education. Brownlee-Williams' research interests include researched-based instructional strategies for P–12 educators, educational policy and compliance, and preservice teacher preparation.

Sarah Bruha wanted to be a teacher since she was young. She grew up visiting her father's classroom and quickly fell in love with the art of teaching and the excitement of learning. Sarah is currently in her third year of teaching 2nd grade at Auburn Elementary. She graduated from Oakland University with an undergraduate degree in elementary education and a master's degree in teacher leadership. Today, Sarah happily opens her doors to other per-service teachers so that they can grow and learn inside the classroom, just as she did while still a preservice teacher.

Colleen Bugaj is a classroom teacher at Auburn Elementary School in the Avondale School District, a public school district headquartered in Auburn Hills, Michigan, in Metro Detroit. She is an educator with more than twenty years of experience, both in California and Michigan. She has held the roles of classroom teacher, mentor teacher, active participator and advocate for Teacher Lab and is a vital member of the Dream Team that brought about the partnership between Avondale Schools and Oakland University. She eagerly supports pre-service teacher candidates, welcoming these burgeoning professionals into her classroom to observe, practice new teaching skills, and begin their teaching practice. Ms. Bugai creates a classroom where kindergarten students feel cherished and begin to understand who they want to be in this world.

Cynthia Carver is an associate professor in the Department of Organizational Leadership at Oakland University where she coordinates graduate programs in educational leadership and teacher leadership. In 2015–2016, she served as scholar in residence at Auburn Elementary, an Avondale/Oakland University partnership school. One of her tasks that year was to convene the Learning & Leading Collaborative, an afterschool meeting of the minds, of which her chapter is a product. Using a learning-focused lens, she is keenly interested in how teachers come to adopt and enact a leaderful presence and practice.

Melanie M. Frizzell has emerged as one of the rising scholarly thinkers on factors contributing to the preparation of teacher education majors and licensure policy. She has recently completed a doctorate in education with a focus on the role of leadership in the preparation on future teachers of color.

Nancy P. Gallavan, Ph.D., is a professor of teacher education in the Department of Teaching and Learning at the University of Central Arkansas, a past president and distinguished member of the Association of Teacher Educators (ATE) and a Kappa Delta Pi (KDP) Eleanor Roosevelt Legacy Chapter inaugural member. With expertise in K-12 education, classroom assessments, curriculum development, cultural competence, social studies education, and teacher self-efficacy, Nancy is active member of AERA, ATE, KDP, NAME, and NCSS.

Contributing to more than 120 publications, Nancy has authored or coauthored *Secrets to Success for Elementary School Teachers, Secrets to Success for Social Studies Teachers, Navigating Cultural Competence: A Compass for Teachers, and Developing Performance Based Assessments* with Corwin Press, edited *Annual Editions: Multicultural Education*, editions 15, 16, and 17 with McGraw-Hill, and coedited ATE Yearbooks XIX–XXVI.

Marcia Hudson began her professional teaching career in the fall of 1987. Fulfilling a childhood dream, she sat elbow-to-elbow with her 7-year-old students for over 22 years, basking in the synergy of learning and teaching. A teacher leader, Marcia has developed a looping program, has created and maintained a leveled literacy library for her school, and has received several awards and recognitions for her classroom accomplishments.

Currently, Marcia serves the Avondale School District as the elementary literacy consultant and the teacher leader/coordinator of the Avondale/Oakland University Partnership. She also designs and coordinates Teacher Lab for the district. Marcia has a degree in elementary education from Oakland University and a master's degree in curriculum and instruction from Michigan State University.

Jennifer Johnson teaches K-5 general music at Auburn Elementary. In addition to teaching music she is the advisor for the Student Leadership Team. The SLT divides their meeting time between developing the leadership skills of its members and sponsoring service projects in and out of school. In 2015, Jenny wrote and received a donorschoose.org grant for a classroom set of ukuleles.

She taught previously for the Harrison Community Schools and Mount Clemens Community Schools. While in Mount Clemens, she was voted as elementary teacher of the year. Jennifer earned her BME from Northern Michigan University and an MME from Central Michigan University. Jennifer welcomes preservice teachers into her classroom each week to encourage them to experience teaching and learning in the arts.

Noran L. Moffett has served in P-12 and higher education roles in a career that includes middle school teacher, high school teacher and administrator and coach to roles of tenured professor, and associate dean at a public and private institution. At the time of submission, Noran is a tenured Professor in the College of Education at Fayetteville State University and he is serves as the Director of the Office of Research Initiatives in the College of Education at Fayetteville State University in fall of 2016. During his tenure in the role of Associate Dean at two institutions, he was the accreditation coordinator. The Educator Preparation Programs at each Intuitional setting successfully completed its NCATE Legacy Accreditation Visit with all standards met. Noran has a passion and commitment to teacher education that includes action research for school leaders and teacher educators, history of education in Historically Black Colleges and Universities and other institutions preparing teacher educators and educational leaders to serve diverse children for our nation's schools and the world. Noran is motivated by the ideal that an "educator in a system of oppression is either an educational revolutionary or an oppressor." His favorite musical group is Earth Wind & Fire and he uses their positive music and lyrics to advance educational philosophy and reflections as an instructor to facilitate the advancement of harmony and peace for humanity and children.

Nurah-Talibah N. Moffett attended George Washington Carver Early College High School where she was a 4-year starter on the varsity tennis team and began dual enrollment at Georgia State University in the second semester of her high school years. She graduated from Georgia State University with a Bachelor of Arts in anthropology and a Minor in history. Currently, she is pursuing the Master of Social Work degree at Clark Atlanta University.

Stacey Pylman is a doctoral student, Ph.D. candidate, in curriculum, instruction, and teacher education at Michigan State University. Her research focuses on mentor teacher learning, mentoring practice, and teacher preparation.

Randi Stanulis is a professor in the Department of Teacher Education at Michigan State University, where she serves as the director of the Launch into Teaching induction program. For more than 20 years she has conducted research on beginning and mentor teacher learning.

Serena Stock is a 1st and 2nd grade teacher at Auburn Elementary. Serena holds an undergraduate degree in elementary education and a master's degree in English language arts and reading diagnosis. During her 25-year tenure, Serena taught one of the longest-running looping programs in Michigan. She has been an integral part of developing Teacher Lab at Auburn and has presented this model at state and national conferences.

Serena helped to bring to and foster the growth of Visible Thinking/Cultures of Thinking throughout the district. She has also been an active part of the Teach to Lead initiative through the U.S. Department of Education. Serena was a member of the planning committee that developed the Oakland University/ Avondale partnership, is now a member of the steering committee, and teaches at the partnership school.

Lindsay Joseph Wexler is a doctoral student, Ph.D. candidate, in curriculum, instruction, and teacher education at Michigan State University. Her areas of interest include teacher preparation, induction, and mentoring.

www.ingramcontent.com/pod-product-compliance
Lightning Source LLC
Chambersburg PA
CBHW030116010526
44116CB00005B/270